Advance Praise For Anger Management For Black Male Teens

"The insights, experiences, and first-hand knowledge of our boys' experiences emanate from Mr. Bourne's pages. He has compiled the research, science, and psychology of the black male experience and framed it in the user-friendly form of story and anecdote. The book provides shared accounts of individuals and their plights, and the author details how they reflect the broader needs of our community and the ails and failures of our systems. Mr. Bourne has crafted a thought-provoking and practical guide for families and educators. A tool for every household and school."

– Noah Tennant, Assistant Superintendent School District of Philadelphia, 2016 Neubauer Fellow

"This is a healing manual. Kenneth did a phenomenal job uncovering the layers of anger. Also, he provides a detailed script to how boys and men can repair themselves to be better all around."

– Jay Barnett, Former Pro Football Player, Author, Marriage, and Family Therapist

"Kenneth Bourne has written a powerful and intimate roadmap for parents of Black boys. His words are a source of truth to promote healing and ultimately the thriving of our communities."

–John Rich, MD, MPH, Director of RUSH BMO Institute for Health Equity

"In this important and praxis-informed new book, Kenneth L. Bourne, Jr. draws on his extensive training and experience working with Black boys and emerging men. Bourne challenges the current status of Black boys in schools—framed by under-expectations and over-discipline—by highlighting perspectives and prescriptions to reinforce and restore the social-emotional well-being of Black adolescent boys. In doing so, he effectively challenges the status quo and offers insightful strategies grounded in holistic approaches that are culturally congruent with the identity of these students. This book is a must-read for parents, social workers, and educators who are committed to wholeness, healing, and community health."

– James Earl Davis, Interim Dean, College of Education & Human Development Bernard C. Watson Chair in Urban Education and Professor of Higher Education, Temple University

"What this book offers is not just an analysis of the expression and catalyst for Anger in teens, particularly in the black community; it offers practical tools to heal and use this emotion in positive ways to move forward. I wish I had access to this when I was a teen."

– Bryan Terrell Clark, Actor, singer/songwriter

"Mr. Bourne has taken on a subject that most of us know about but rarely talk about. This book explores the volatile temperament that men display and offers sound advice on how to help your son and you understand it. If you have a black teenage boy in your house, this is a must-read."

– David Hardy, Distinguished Senior Fellow Commonwealth Foundation

"Kenneth Bourne has authored a brilliant, much-needed blueprint for parents and caregivers of Black boys to creatively help boys and young men manage their anger and emotions. Bourne provides parents with tools, based on brain science research, that will help enable the power of choice and control of emotions in the lives of Black boys. Meshing his personal story and experiences with his training as a sociologist, along with his love of Black boys, Bourne has created a manifesto for the health, healing, and well-being of Black boys for parents who are desperately searching for help to support their sons navigate today's daunting, dangerous adolescent terrain."

– Shawn Dove, Founder, Corporation for Black Male Achievement, Manager Partner, New Profit

"I taught in communities of color for 15 years, working primarily with young Black men. As a white woman and an outsider, I wish I had had a book like this in my early years of teaching to help explain what I was seeing and to offer practical, useful, effective suggestions for how to work with teenagers. Kenneth provides insight and clarity to the struggles many young Black men face— but he also gives helpful and necessary tools for any concerned teacher or parent to try. Kenneth's ideas are grounded in his deep belief in compassion and his understanding of healing the whole person from within. His exercises invite conversation and reflection while promoting change. I am excited to implement them in my own classroom."

– Sara Flounders, MDiv, Latin instructor

"Kenneth Bourne's book is an honest, refreshing guide for anyone supporting young Black males navigating their world. The feelings associated with racism, oppression, injustice, social pressures, and internal and external threats are real – and there is no denying that here. Bourne is relatable and resourceful, using his personal and professional wisdom to coach and inspire Black youth to build their emotional intelligence and safely respond to feelings underlying anger – especially sadness, hurt, fear, and shame. From emotional regulation strategies to meditation, building self-acceptance, and identifying and communicating feelings, this book is full of valuable lessons, tools, and encouragement. This is an easy-to-read, real, and practical guide, informed by advances in science, psychology, clinical social work, and the movement for social and racial justice. Anyone who reads this book is sure to be inspired and feel hopeful about protecting the futures of young Black men and creating safer, braver spaces where they may feel empowered to be themselves and discover their own strengths and true worth."

– Jennifer Wilson, PhD, LCSW

"Kenneth Bourne has written a critically important book. Anger Management for Teens doesn't merely offer tools to adults who care. This roadmap to well-being explores the underlying causes of anger and lays bare inequity and systemic issues that often remain unaddressed in such texts. Kenn recognizes that instead of addressing the systems affecting our teens, we often address the symptoms, leaving our youth to feel that something is inherently wrong with them. This book is infused with deep care. Kenn stands firmly in the knowing that there is nothing wrong with them, you, or anyone else. He reaches out a loving hand of support, wanting nothing but wellness, happiness, and the recognition of the light within for all. An important roadmap to well-being indeed!"

–Caverly Morgan, author of The Heart of Who We Are: Realizing Freedom Together and A Kids Book About Mindfulness. Founder of Peace in Schools

Anger Management
For
Black Male Teens

A Practical Guide On How To Help Your Teen
Manage Their Emotions

Written By: Kenneth L. Bourne Jr., LSW

www.bourneanew.com

ISBN: 979-8-9877693-6-2

Editing and Layout by I A.M. Editing, Ink

Contents

🎁A FREE GIFT TO OUR READERS🎁

A complete holistic affirmation guide for Black boys and men with nine sections totaling 225 affirmations. Visit bourneanew.com/services-resources

Black Male Affirmation Guide

Introduction

The biggest problem that Black boys face is no longer the attack on their race. It is not their lack of vulnerability, the unending discrimination, or the monstrous statistics and odds stacked against them. It is, on the contrary, the war with themselves. It is their mental makeup. The limiting beliefs they have come to accept as Black men that developed over their lifetimes.

I hate to be blunt about this, but you must hear it. The limiting beliefs that have been violently and systemically intertwined within the lives of Black boys are killing them.

Put yourself in their shoes for the next couple of sentences. The following sentences are all phrases I have heard... you are the worst race walking this earth! You are the angriest, most violent, unproductive, and most irrelevant race on this earth. You march the streets angrily shouting, "Black lives matter," when your friend gets murdered by another Black man but perpetuate the hurt by killing the next. You are the silent mastermind of the most heinous crimes ever committed on this planet.

Many Black male teens feel as if they have no chance at any sort of life beyond what they've experienced - that they are unprogressive and don't deserve a place among the top people in the world. As a Black male teen, there is no escaping this reality. The constant feeling of being a nuisance due to the color of your skin. History and present-day tells them that the color of their skin stands for everything that is wrong with humanity. You know it, but you choose ignorance every time you function as if this is not true. Whether you are in America, Asia, or even our own Africa, the message remains the same – that they are subservient to all other races because white bodies are the supreme standard by which all other bodies are measured.

How would you feel if the world around you consistently told you, in so many ways, that your existence is useless? You would be angry too! As we Black folks say, your ears would be burning, which is a saying that we reference when one is being talked about to another.

We all know the statistics and the reality of Black adolescent males, yet, very few of us know resources that offer coaching on how to help them. There are and always will be social and outreach programs that target Black youth, but these measures often suffer from a lack of funding, public awareness, and short staff. Social service-related programs often lack Black male leadership and staff. The few Black male-specific support services often lack public awareness and social respect. The Center for Black male Educator Development is a great resource for Black males who are looking to join the teaching profession, which remains overwhelmingly white and grew even whiter, claims an Education Weekly article ("Still Mostly White and Female: New Federal Data on the Teaching Profession," 2020).

I am Kenneth Bourne, a licensed social worker in Philadelphia with an organization that seeks to restore the well-being of Black boys and men. I have heard these same words my whole life. I have been cornered and bullied by White folks. I have been emotionally scarred for being Black. I have been interrogated and accused of committing a crime simply because another person said so. I have had to fight my entire life in hopes that fighting will increase my chances of living longer. I have been kicked out of schools and physically assaulted by teachers, to mention a few.

Hence, none of the statements mentioned above are new to me. I understand your fury and why you are about to lose a fuse over my derogatory statements. These derogatory words, statistics, and disturbing media reports are why you are here.

You are here because you are looking for answers, hope, and resources to address the emotional well-being of Black male adolescents. More importantly, you are here because you understand that the well-being of Black boys/men in America is literally a discussion of life and death. Suicide has increased from the third to now being the second leading cause of death in Black adolescents. According to the American Academy of Child and Adolescent Psychiatry, compared to all other racial groups, it has increased by 60%, faster than any other racial or ethnic group. "Suicide is a growing problem among Black Americans, and young Black males account for most of those deaths" (Joe et al., 2018). As babies, "[b]oys are socialized to reject vulnerability, toughen up, and 'be a man (Smith & Patton, 2016). The past and current reality have likely shown you that our people are in need. Still, there is a severe lack of educational resources specifically tailored for the development of Black boys.

As a parent, caregiver, teacher, activist, or simply put- a person who cares, you fear our Black teens are not growing old. Parents have told me multiple times that they are afraid of losing their. Teachers are tired of burying their Black male students. Community members are growing weary of the consistent headlines that highlight the loss of our Black male teens to anger, the streets, drugs, and prison.

In this book, I'll provide a way to assist Black male teenagers more holistically. I'm not here to lecture or preach to you. I'm sure you're already sick of getting that all the time. Instead, I'm here to help you as you try to help them hike their mountain. You'll learn how to help them manage their feelings from the inside out. You'll learn to identify the root of anger, understand the message anger is trying to pass, and help them express it healthily.

By the end of this book, you'll feel more equipped to help Black male teens become more balanced using the exercises and lessons in this book. You'll be provided with theories, resources, and tools to help them handle their emotions and channel them positively. You may even notice a change as there is a possibility that they can become a happier and healthier version of themselves.

This is not just a book. It is a well-being roadmap to a better overall quality of life. It should be used as a both read and experienced separately and then together as parent and child or teacher and student so forth. All I ask is that you take the well-being of Black adolescents seriously. Open your heart to understanding and your mind to receiving.

Some information within this book is not new, and I hope it sensitizes you in a way that rids the numbness that we all have come to expect as normal when viewing the lives of Black male adolescents. This book is a resource for but not limited to Black boys, clinicians, teachers, parents, educators, caregivers, coaches, CEOs, record label companies, the tech industry, and all the spaces in between where Black boys/men inhabit.

With practical advice and easy-to-do exercises, this book is designed to give you the tools to help them change their life. Ultimately, it's up to them to use them! The tools you'll learn may help you calm your mind and respond from the best parts of yourselves. Helping Black male teens learn how to effectively communicate their thoughts and feelings without exploding in rage is essential. Together, we'll go through exercises to build self-confidence, self-esteem, and resilience.

Now I know what you're thinking: That's a lot of things to learn! But can I let you in on a secret? These skills and tools don't take much time to learn at all. You're probably already even familiar with a few of them. Simply taking a few minutes daily to practice one skill at a time can have massive benefits. Just try it. You'll want to learn more as you use these skills and see their effects.

Growing up, I was constantly in trouble. I always got into fights, some so intense I was detained by police, received multiple suspensions, and was even expelled from a school. As a Black man who grew up in the hood of Philly, I know what it means to live as a Black teenager in America. Like them, I struggled with and frankly still struggle with the anger inside me, feeling hopeless and helpless. Again, there are no quick fixes, and we must begin to see this issue on a continuum, where the emotion will always be there, but our relationship to it changes with time. By using healing-centered engagement strategies, holistic modalities, therapy, and studying myself and others, I slowly began to understand the potential causes of my anger. I used the techniques in this book to channel my anger into positive and creative endeavors.

As a licensed social worker, I've worked with many Black boys and men, helping them achieve a better quality of life. I am passionate about sharing my knowledge and experience with you, as I know this information has the potential to save lives. As someone who understands the pain and struggle and has made it to the other side, I'm here to encourage you as you help others overcome destructive behavioral patterns.

When you finish reading and working through this book, I hope you'll feel more comfortable helping Black male teenagers handle stress and frustration. I hope you will help them to cope and restore well-being as they continue to explore their inner landscape.

With that in mind, work through the book chapter by chapter. Each chapter contains practical information; some have anecdotes from clients I have once worked with, and others contain detailed exercises. Complete any worksheet you find and practice the exercises. You can try them out on your own or with others. Keep a notebook or journal as you read. The journal will be a free space for you to reflect on the lessons, and explore your feelings as you may uncover and release some emotions.

Society has conditioned men to see emotional expression as a sign of weakness. However, suppressing and bottling up emotions can cause them to explode or leak out in unpleasant ways. So, the first step to emotional intelligence and controlling anger is gaining the language and ability to communicate and express healthily. But before you express your feelings, you must learn to identify them. That is where we begin.

In Chapter One, we'll answer the question, "Why Is He So Angry?" Here, we'll try to define emotions and feelings and some potential causes of anger in Black male teens, so you can start building the skills for understanding. You've got this! Now, let's get started.

I'm reaching out in search of therapy for my 16-year-old son, who has been having more and more issues in school lately. When I inquire with him verbally, he isn't very responsive; however, it is evident that his emotions are very up and down. I want to discuss and possibly make an action plan to help my son. I want him to be the best version of himself, and as of late, I don't feel he is. Any help you can provide is greatly appreciated.

~Concerned Parent

1

Why Is He So Angry?

What Does Anger Look Like For Black Male Teens?

Have you ever asked yourself that question as a parent, care-giver, or educator? One might answer by saying: "When my son is yelling, cursing, and not communicating with me." Or like "Fighting, punching objects, and displaying disruptive be-havior." If you have never asked yourself this question, take some time now and see what comes up for you.

Is it a description of the symptoms? Or characteristics of people who once upset or irritated you? So, what is anger? While most people can agree that anger is an emotion, emotions are complex, and defining them on a deeper level is important for learning how to manage anger. Defining emotion is also neces-sary to give us direction and clarity as we move throughout this book.

Emotion and feeling are used interchangeably, yet they are not the same. Here are the definitions that I use and come from my own knowledge and research.

To answer the question "What is anger?" let's take some time to define emotions and how anger shows up as one of them. For clarification, I do not have a clear definition, nor does the field of neurobiology, interpersonal neurobiology, neuroscience, positive psychology, etc., regarding emotion. Emotions are complex, and while you can Google to find an answer, it does not seem to satisfy one's understanding. If you were to Google "define emotion," you would get many results. Some definitions will mention that emotions are either instinctive or intuitive. Other definitions say it is a state of mind or a mental reaction. Still, these do not explain emotions and provide conflicting results. We must define feeling and emotion as they are foundational principles for this book. Emotion and feeling are used interchangeably, yet they are not they same. Here are the definitions that I use. I must add that these definitions are from my own knowledge and research.

E·mo·tion: A complex reaction system involving the brain, body, people, and the environment helping to create the subjective experience of an individual and evokes motion.

Feel·ing: Feelings give rise to emotions as a complex intrinsic process that may or may not be linked to emotions and involve the brain, body, people, and the environment.

See the diagram below of how I argue the process works:

Feeling $\longrightarrow$ Emotion $\longrightarrow$ Emotion

I have seen firsthand some of the harm that may fuel Black male teens' anger. I have seen this as a first-generation college graduate, a former school social worker in Philadelphia, a director of teens in Camden, New Jersey, a social worker at a clinic in a high-needs area, and a community intervention specialist at Drexel University. Anger is a secondary emotion, often masking other underlying feelings. These feelings include sadness, hurt, fear, and shame. Underlying feelings can become too much without the resources or tools needed to work through them. As a result, humans instinctively do what they first learned when they experienced anger. For male Black teens, this will mimic the motions and behaviors presented at time of anger.

The early learned lesson of anger is familiar and comfortable. Black male teens tend to disengage through anger as a protective mechanism. Their perspective is that they are protecting themselves from further hurt. Yet, they are stunting their own growth. Anger has become a prominent place within them. They have learned to navigate this location with ease. Outside the uncharted territories of Black male teens' comfort zones and neighborhoods lies the changed man both they want, and you want them to be.

In later chapters, I will explain the connection between the brain and anger, but for now- here is what you should understand when it comes to understanding emotions and feelings: no one knows what they exactly are. An important detail is that the word emotion comes from the Latin root *emovere*. *Emovere* means to move or move out. An emotion is a process that evokes motion. As we dive deeper into looking at anger, we often attempt to define it by naming its symptoms or descriptions rooted in some form of action. The simple fact is we all experience something within us, almost instinctively. It is this inner exploration that I seek to help explain and help others understand.

When it comes to anger for Black teens, we must have the conversation contextually. For Black teens, anger is never understood as an emotion. Instead, it is diagnosed, criminalized, and used against them as a weapon. I have worked with many Black teens who struggled with anger because that was all they knew to name. No one is helping them process or understand what they feel inside. Black teens lack opportunities to embark on a journey of self-fulfillment.

Anger for Black teens has been commodified. Anger is sold back to Black teens via rap music, video games, social media, television, and movies. Taking a deeper look at rap music, for example, a rapper's credibility is closely linked to his/her ability to partake in violence and their street reputation in their community. It is common for a high-profile gang member to quickly climb the charts of fame in the music industry. Worst of all, the sensationalization of violence has become mixed in with Black culture. If one does not subscribe to the unwritten rules of anger, they are subjected to the unwritten consequences (i.e., bullying, interpersonal violence, gun violence, etc.).

Unconsciously, Black teens are taught anger. In their reality, anger is the only acceptable emotion, and violence is the way to express it. These learned lessons come from seeing or being in a physical altercation in the neighborhood, receiving a whooping or beating from caregivers that misnomer it as discipline, or the deeper-rooted violence Black bodies have experienced in America.

Working with clients, I have seen first-hand how anger masks their true feelings or emotions, making naming and expressing the underlying feelings more difficult. Systems like schools put so much effort and resources into addressing symptoms of anger (i.e., disruptive behavior) that partaking in anger is the quickest and easiest way to be seen. Think about it, when was the last time you checked up on the kid who seems to have everything going right for them? But I can guarantee that you can quickly recall a memory of a teen who displayed disruptive behavior.

In spaces where Black male teens are, you'll hear common sayings like, "caring makes you weak" and "a real man doesn't express sadness or fear." These statements breed a society of emotionless Black teens. With no rights to ownership of their emotions, they lack the skills and abilities to work on them, so they turn to anger as the only acceptable emotional outlet to survive. Not having the skills to manage their anger effectively or other feelings makes them susceptible to and unprotected from the dangers of this world. The masked feelings—such as sadness, fear, or guilt— buried within can cause a teen to feel vulnerable. Yet, vulnerability is seen as a weakness or unsafe within respected environments, so they hide it.

The additional emotions that can exist underneath anger can be seen within a feelings wheel. I use a feelings wheel or mood meter when working one-on-one with Black male tees to help them begin naming the feelings that may be giving rise to the emotions that they are feeling. One resource I like to use is Yale's mood meter because it helps them not only name what they are feeling but also recognize if it is a pleasant or unpleasant feeling and whether they feel energized or depleted.

In helping Black male teens develop the necessary skills and understand that there are more emotionally expressive ways of being than just anger: hurt, hostile, angry, selfish, hateful, critical, skeptical, irritated, jealous, frustrated, sarcastic, and distant, we will use the analogy of an iceberg.

Think of anger as the top section of an iceberg, the part you can see. This part of the iceberg represents the outward motions and behaviors of anger. These are the symptoms commonly seen and diagnosed, misunderstood, and labeled. These outward motions and behaviors may look like yelling, harming others, and explosiveness, to name a few. These are all the things we can see as they are above water. They are often not looked at as cues to something more profound.

However, the most substantial and strongest part of an iceberg is the portion beneath the water; these are the feelings that are not so easy to spot. Although anger is displayed outwardly, other feelings are hidden beneath the surface. By being curious and exploring what is beneath the surface, you can gain insight into their anger and may be able to help support them in identifying their needs. But before you begin exploring what lies beneath the iceberg, you must make sure that you are taking all the proper precautionary measures. The following section is an activity you should complete for yourself first, and then with them to help ensure everyone's safety, as exploring the unchartered territory of a Black male's emotions can be intense.

Creating A Safety Plan

Before abruptly diving in, safety should be the priority before navigating the waters of emotional and relational health. I want you to please take extra caution as you begin to navigate one's feelings and emotions, but more importantly, Black male teen emotions. Creating a safety plan can help you with this. One must understand that discussing emotions can be triggering and potentially do more harm without proper precautions.

Understanding that our brains and bodies process, store, and recall emotions on their own, we do not have a say about what gets stored and where within our brains and bodies during a traumatic incident. As a result, one must explore these areas very carefully. Lakeside Global Institute (LGI) defines a safety plan as follows:

A predetermined list of ways a person can mentally or physically ensure they remain safe, especially if a topic, activity, or environment is perceived as potentially dangerous or threatening. Safety plans are a list of specific mental or physical actions that support both the permission and power for individuals to maintain their own safety.[1]
(Enhancing Trauma Awareness Curriculum, pg. 20).

There are two basic types of safety plans: 1) internal and 2) external. An internal safety plan explores the variety of ways a per-

---

1. Lakeside Global Institute Enhancing Trauma Awareness Curriculum, pg. 20.

son can remain present and calm mentally. An external safety plan explores the ways a person can ensure physical safety for themselves. Please refer to the chart below to help create a safety plan.

Safety Plan Example: Internal

Name one thing I can see. Name one thing I can smell. Name one thing I can touch. Name one thing I can taste.	Repeat these phrases: I am safe. I am loved. I have the power to care for myself. I am not in danger.
Intentionally feel my draws touch my skin Breathe. Slowly. Deeply. Remind myself of the date and time	What am I feeling? Where am I feeling it? How can I regain a sense of calm?

Safety Plan Example: External

Note where the exits are. Sit near the door. Notice who is in the room. Tell someone you trust when you start to feel unsafe.	Sit near someone you feel safe being close to. Go to the bathroom. Sit in a spot where you feel safest. Decide a safe place to go.
Doodle. Quietly hum. Tap. Think about what you want to eat afterward.	Drink water. Exit the room. Refuse to speak. Close your eyes for a few seconds.

The safety plan helps provides protection and security as you begin to help them with their emotions. For example, when working with John, a teen who was told he was diagnosed with intermittent explosive disorder regarding his anger, I knew that I needed to create a safe way for him to express his anger and for me to deal with it when he got angry. Deep down, he felt that he did not have anger issues but was never taught safe forms of expression or given the language to communicate his feelings. I had him take an index card and make four sections (drawing a horizontal line across the center and a vertical line from top to bottom, making the letter "t"). Then fill in each section accordingly, just like the charts above.

I must add that there is no universal safety plan. It would be best to customize and tailor the safety plan to what they feel contributes to helping them feel safe, aware of triggers, and stay in the present moment. He was able to carry this index card with him and refer to it as needed as he navigated his day. His tremendous behavioral progress, from receiving daily demerits for a week to receiving none the next week, led to him making copies of his safety plan and giving them to each of his teachers. This created a community that was invested in his safety rather than punitive measures.

Another activity that you can do with Black male teens is called "safety pin." To complete this activity, you will need a safety pin and various colored beads. Have them think of something or someone positive in their life that almost always brings them joy when they see or think of it. Next, allow them to select two to three colors that will remind them of those joyous memories. Once their beads are chosen, open the safety pin, slide the beads through, and pin the safety pin on their shirt or backpack.

Once a safety plan has been created, you can move to the iceberg activity. I strongly suggest making the iceberg activity some sort of extra credit assignment or incentivizing it in some way. This allows their brains to release the feel-good hormone as they work through their emotions and feelings.

YOU TRY IT!

Iceberg Activity Practice

The goal of this activity is to help figure out what is beneath a teen's anger.

Search for the words "anger iceberg," and you will find many helpful images. I like the infographic from the therapistaid.com website, but most are an excellent place to start. Remember, the tip of the iceberg is how one outwardly expresses anger, while the portion beneath the water is all the other factors at play and can be the root cause of the anger. Take some time to research this iceberg before moving forward in this book. A good example is the anger iceberg found on therapistaid.com as a therapy worksheet.

The idea of an iceberg is commonly used within interdisciplinary spaces that focus on people impacted by trauma. Lakeside Global Institute (LGI) does a great job explaining and showing how people affected by trauma can be compared to an iceberg.

LGI explains that people can be compared with an iceberg in the following ways:

The visible parts above the surface become labels and are categorized as outward behaviors.

Iceberg Analogy

Outward Behavior
(the part you can see)

Real power is below the surface where emotional and relational health lies unseen.

Emotional Health
(self-esteem, moral character, self confidence, self image)

Relational Health
(love, fairness, trust & trustworthiness, power)

The strength of the layers under the water determines the real strength of the iceberg.

Image appear by permission of Lakeside Global Institute, Enhancing Trauma Awareness Curriculum, (2006).

- Many people focus on assessing and addressing outward behaviors, often without considering the underlying causes.

- The strength of an iceberg lies beneath the surface.

- Human beings have two layers that exist beneath the surface: the first being emotional health, followed by relational health at the very bottom.

- Though these layers are different, they are interconnected.

- The emotional health layer represents the inner subjective world of a person (i.e., degrees of self-esteem, self-awareness, self-confidence, self-discipline, etc.).

- The relational health layer represents how a person engages in healthy relationships with others.

- The top of the iceberg (outward behaviors) is the result of the health in the two underlying layers.

- The words in the lower part of the iceberg represent undercurrents in the process of anger. These areas within the iceberg represent the damage from the relational health area or emotional health area.

- The rugged edges can potentially be smoothed over through loving, safe, and consistent healthy relationships.

- When parents and caregivers are aware of the rugged edges and are intentional about repairing the chips, they can ensure a greater probability of Black teens reaching their full potential.

Below, I have a blank iceberg, and I challenge you to do this activity on yourself and then with the Black teens in your life. Remember, the tip of the iceberg is all the ways in which one outwardly expresses anger, while the portion beneath the water is all the other factors at play that go unnoticed but have detrimental effects on their health.

Image appear by permission of Lakeside Global Institute, Enhancing Trauma Awareness Curriculum, (2006).

You may have said this yourself or heard others say, "these kids are out-of-control!" This idea is that teens with serious anger issues are consumed with anger. Once this label is prescribed, you will notice that people stop showing compassion for them. They will begin to see them as adult individuals who are defiant, aggressive, or violent-hence behavioral problems in school. Misunderstanding anger can have unintended consequences for your teen because they are no longer receiving love in ways that support their development. Some unintended consequences may be participating in risky behaviors and abusing substances to cope with their strong emotions.

However, let's change that narrative and not allow anyone to define your son, student, relative, or loved one. By reading this book, you are trusting me to give you fundamental strategies that will play a vital role in helping them thrive. You are seeking guidance in understanding their emotions in hopes of not losing him to violence, the streets, drugs, and all the other structural mishaps that plague our communities. Black male teens *should* be angry because systemically, their current society is set up for them to fail by creating redlined neighborhoods (i.e., the hood, trenches, etc.) with no access to healthy foods, safety, equitable education, and life skills. How do I know this? Because I am from these neighborhoods, and so is my family. That is why you are here; you know the power of having a strong mind and body that can control emotions. We have the unique opportunity to develop this power further and save our Black teens. In the following chapters, we will define potential common causes and factors of Black male teenage anger.

Key Takeaways:

- The word emotion is derived from the Latin word emovere. Emovere means to move or move out. Essentially emotion is the process that evokes motion. In trying to define "anger," we suggest symptoms or descriptions rooted in some form of motion or drive to do something.

- Anger is often the emotion Black teens are taught to express.

- Exploring the underlying causes of anger can help Black teens identify their needs.

- Anger in America has been used as a systemic tool to label our Black teens, further causing more harm and justification for violence against them.

- Emotions and feelings are what make us human and should not be punished.

- In discussing one's emotions, the words right or wrong should not be mentioned because there is no right or wrong way to feel.

- Healthy, safe, loving relationships can help smooth out the rugged parts and restore well-being.

In the next chapter, we will uncover some potential environments in which seeds of anger are planted to see how they grow into the outward behaviors you see within your Black teen.

2

What Makes Him So Angry?

Hi Mr. Bourne,

I found you on PsychologyToday.com. I am reaching out to see if you can help me. I have two sons, but I am only calling about my oldest. His name is Q. Bartton. He is 12 and going on 13 and has anger issues. My situation is a lot, and a lot is happening. My son is becoming harder to control. When he is angry, he seems like a different person; where he hits on his younger brother, hits me, breaks things, yells, screams, etc. I have tried everything.

Sincerely,
A Concerned Mother

Small. Skinny. A dark brown hue with curly hair and big eyes greeted me on a video conference call. He was accompanied by his mother kneeling behind his chair with a smile on her face. He looked defeated, tired, as if he had just lost a great battle—the war with himself. Mom began introducing her son and explaining why she felt he would benefit from talking to someone who looked like him, could express love and kindness, and was a man. As she explained her reasoning for our call, he began shaking his head in disagreement with his mother's interpretation of his anger. Once his mother exited the room, allowing for privacy and authenticity, I started our conversation by checking in with him.

I began by inquiring about his day, the food he ate, and anything else he wanted to share. Like all my Black adolescent clients, his response was, "I'm good." This saying is vital to recognize when analyzing and addressing the emotions of Black teens. If they respond with "I'm good" after you inquire about their day, mood, etc., your following response will determine the foundation of the relationship and dictate how the rest of the interaction will go. The phrase "I'm good" is a very efficient test that helps them decide if an adult cares or if it's just a formality. If you want to begin a more meaningful connection to have a more profound impact, this is your one and only opportunity to do so.

Your response as their caregiver, teacher, etc., matters twofold. On one end of the continuum, your answer will communicate how much you care; on the other, it will set the foundation for a healthy relationship. Black teen boys learn early on that no one truly cares. Whether this is true or not does not necessarily matter. What matters is how a person feels. If you can connect or speak to how they feel (i.e., the subjective experience), you have a better chance of making an impact. In response to "I'm good," you must go a step further to decode what the word "good" means for them. Within the context of a conversation, the word "good" can have many different meanings for Black teen boys. One way to effectively try and figure out what "good" means for them is to use the mood meter discussed in chapter one. Here are how my conversations typically go with my clients:

Kenn: "What's up! As I stated before, being able to serve where God allows is my passion. I truly care about your well-being and want to help you wherever you need it. With that, let's start with checking in. My check-ins typically look like me asking about how you are feeling, your day, the foods you ate, anything fun or not so fun that happened, and anything else you would like to share."

Client: "Okay...umm, I'm doing good...my day was good. Didn't really do much today. And umm, I had cereal this morning."

Kenn: "Okay. I appreciate you sharing. And I'm going to need more information than that, my guy! First, help me understand what "good" means for you because "good" is not a feeling. If you need help naming your feelings, let me know, and we can refer to a feelings chart or mood meter to help you. Have you ever heard of a feelings chart? It is okay if you haven't, but it can help us start to name our feelings/emotions...."

I won't bore you all with the rest of the conversation, but that is my go-to response when working with Black male teens. Never ask any teenager how they are feeling and accept "good" as a response. As you can see, just from my checking in with them, the door of potential swung open to a room full of opportunities to explore more. This small and simple technique makes room for a big and complex foundation.

Now, let's get back to Q. Bartton. After introductions and check-ins within our first hour-long session, I discovered that Q. Bartton's anger was rooted deep within the relational health area of the iceberg and some areas connected to the emotional health region. His father was abusive to his mother, which he had witnessed on many occasions. He was also getting bullied in school. They ended up moving across the country, without his father, to an area where his mother felt safe and could be around family. The overwhelming conflicting emotions of loving and missing his father yet despising his father's behavior resulted in him being someone he did not want to be.

Besides being bullied, Q. Bartton's self-esteem, self-image, love, and trust were drastically affected. Q. Bartton told me he disliked getting angry but could not control it. He wished to have a better handle on it. He also recognized that his behaviors mimicked his father's, which also fueled his anger because he shared that he never wanted to be like him.

In Q. Bartton's case, he unconsciously learned his father's behavior and became a bully to his siblings at home to cope with the bullying he was receiving at school. His outward behaviors of hitting, yelling, destroying things, and saying hurtful things mirrored his reality of living with an abusive parent. Unfortunately, as a Black male teen, his learned behaviors can have life-altering effects. America has not been kind in the past or present regarding Black men and our mental health.

To illustrate this point, I will reflect on an event that can be triggering for some, so I encourage you to grab your safety plans and keep them nearby. Walter Wallace Jr., a 27-year-old Black man, was murdered by police in West Philadelphia. There has been evidence via recorded previous phone calls and conversations in which the family called 9-1-1 asking for the ambulance, not the police. When police arrived, Walter had been experiencing a mental illness emergency in which his mother could be heard and seen shouting that he was "mental" before the cops murdered him.

The family had called for help many times before the police arrived. There is a history and numerous examples of how Black men's mental health struggles are perceived as a threat and something that needs to be met with great violence. Q. Bartton just wanted to be a 12-year-old boy who did not have to choose between his parents but a kid who liked video games, sports, and trips to the park.

Referring to the iceberg analogy, we can see that Q. Bartton's anger was rooted in both emotional and relational health areas. His emotional health was suffering compared to a 12-year-old who did not have to worry about his safety being compromised by someone he loved. He shared that he loved going to the park with his father. His love for his father made him question his moral character and his identity as a growing teen who aspired to one day have a family of his own. *How could I love and miss someone I do not aspire to be like? How do I confidently express myself without hurting others? Is this what I look like? Where is my example of a healthy relationship? Is this how I'm supposed to communicate to others that I love?* These are all questions he struggled with, and his developing mind was not equipped to answer and, quite frankly, should not have to.

In addition, his relational health was completely shattered. Not having the opportunity to figure out the complexity of healthy interaction with others at home, and in school coincides with the struggles in developing his own identity. Instead of learning his own voice, he was too busy trying to quiet the yelling of his parents. Therefore, a potential root cause of his anger can be found in his upbringing.

Systemic Reasons Behind Black Teen Anger

There may be many causes of one's anger. At Rutgers University School of Social Work, I was taught that the personal is political, meaning that issues that are typically considered personal should be considered in the political sector. This is true for Black male teens, specifically regarding emotions. They are not afforded the opportunities to freely feel and express themselves, leaving their emotions to be shaped by political and structural systems like racism. Some contributing factors to Black teen anger may be:

- Racism
- Societal pressures
- Transition into adulthood
- Trying to fit in
- Identity and purpose
- Seeking to be accepted and included
- Struggling to make friends
- Academic problems
- Not having resources to develop who they feel they are
- Not being able just to be a Black boy and having to take on adult responsibilities
- Grief and loss
- The feeling of being misunderstood and not belonging

Here's the thing, teens are not much different than adults. We are all trying to figure ourselves out. Even adults deal with similar issues when they become angry when something doesn't go their way. Maybe you get mad at yourself when you don't understand a concept or feel you are misunderstood. Or when your hard work is not hard enough. When you have a hard time reaching a goal, you might become frustrated. That frustration can lead to anger. What about when someone treats you in a way that you don't like (i.e., bullying) or how you used to get angry (and potentially still do) with your parents when you thought one of their rules was unfair and that they didn't understand you? The worst is when you are blamed for something you didn't do. More on the adolescent brain will be discussed in later chapters.

Rawhide Youth Services cites that 40% of teens admit to feeling some sort of anger and that five common triggers of anger for teens are:

- Oppression
- Stress
- Social Confusion
- Hunger
- Puberty
- (https://www.rawhide.org/blog/wellness/teen-anger-aggression-causes-treatment/)

As teens develop, they gain more self-awareness. Learning to be self-aware can help teens cultivate self-control when they are angry. So, when we punish teens regarding their anger, essentially, we are punishing them for having an emotion and not being alive long enough to develop more self-awareness. That doesn't seem right, does it?

Dealing with an angry teen is a frustrating experience that may leave the adult feeling as if they're trying to fight fire with fire. The saying "it takes a village to raise a child," while true, I believe another African proverb to be more accurate and captures the reality of Black male teen anger: "the child who is not embraced by the village will burn it down to feel its warmth." This African proverb beautifully captures the outward behaviors of our Black teens. In analyzing 250+ coaching inquiries for my services, a recurring theme was the idea of seeking acceptance. Their reality is that they do not feel embraced by their communities or society, which ignites the fire to burn what's around them. When they did not feel accepted or included, they seemed cold-hearted, making it easy to not care about destroying anything in their path because it allows them to feel the warmth, even if it means destroying things in the process.

Keeping in mind some of our discussions in chapter one, the so-called "bad" kids receive all the attention, whether good or bad, it is attention that they typically do not receive as they are often overlooked. Some teens need more help learning how to manage their emotions and cope with stress. Other teens experience intense anger as a symptom of a mental health issue, traumatizing life experience, or simply from the stress and brain plasticity of adolescence.

You're probably wondering how I teach them self-awareness so they can begin self-regulating before it's too late and the targeted violent systems deem them unfit for society. One way to do this is by practicing presence in the form of meditation. Practicing presence can be applied in many ways, but for the purposes of this book, I found that meditation works well with Black male teens. Teens are naturally curious and so helping them turn that curiosity inward to explore their inner being was something they enjoyed. Now, if you are working in a school or with a large capacity of Black male teens, the idea of doing meditation with a bunch of teens may initially trigger laughter.

Here is a hard truth that you need to accept, you must believe in the ability and potential of something like meditation for your students to follow. This means that the whole organization needs to be on one accord regarding the well-being of those they serve. Specifically, for a school or organization that works with many Black male teens, there needs to be a physical space that is separate from the classroom.

This space seeks to allow Black male teens to safely express their emotions and naturally work through them. This physical space must mirror calmness to their bodies, including but not limited to meditation-type music playing, affirmations and breathing exercises on the walls, soft furniture, fidgets, etc. This physical space is no different than going to a massage therapy appointment and feeling relaxed because that the physical space has a calming vibe.

In later chapters, I will teach you about the adolescent brain, but for now, all you need to understand is that teens spend most of their adolescent years in the emotional region of their brain. Teaching them about their brains and bodies through meditation is how I help them become self-aware.

Meditation is used to train one's awareness. It has the ability of transformation. You may be wondering how to get an angry teen to sit and meditate. My reality is that once you build a trusting relationship with them, they are more willing to follow your lead. I discuss how to build healthy relationships in chapter nine. Dr. Dan Siegel created a tool called the wheel of awareness. You can learn more about this technique on his website at https://drdansiegel.com/wheel-of-awareness/.

YOU TRY IT!

Wheel Of Awareness Activity Practice

If you think of a bike wheel, you can imagine the center of the wheel along with the many spokes attached to the rim. The rim represents all things we can be aware of. The wheel in this example is broken into four different sections. Dr. Dan Siegel labels them as our five, sixth, seventh, and eighth senses. The first quadrant is the five senses are our senses of touch, taste, smell, sight, and hearing. The second quadrant is the sixth sense is the perception of sensations inside the body, such as muscles, bones, heart, respiratory systems, etc. He also calls this *introception*. Within the third quadrant, the seventh sense, lies mental activities such as thoughts, memories, emotions, worries you might have, etc. Lastly, we have the eighth sense, a relational sense, which is our relationship with others (i.e., family, friends, people, etc.).

In continuation of explaining the diagram, the spoke represents our attention. It takes us from the hub (center) to the rim. Depending on where we place the spoke is where our attention goes. The center of the wheel, also known as the hub, represents the space of knowing. Within this space, we are simply aware of things. This space is fillable depending on where we give our attention. If you want to practice this, go to https://drdansiegel.com/wheel-of-awareness/, where he provides different variations of this practice and guides you through it.

I practice this guided practice with my teenage clients. My clients report how after doing this practice, they can see how they are in more control than they once realized. Moving their attention wherever they want helps them know that they have the power and control versus their anger having the power and control. When they became angry, they realized that all their attention was laser-focused on one thing (whatever bothered them). Using Q. Bartton, for example, after just four sessions, he realized that he focused so much on not being like his dad that he was becoming him. With practice, they realized that by changing their awareness and the direction of their attention, they could also change how they were feeling.

Another important aspect of this wheel is the hub. The hub is a mental space in your brain where you can bring your thoughts and emotions to awareness. Think of the hub as a glass cup, an empty space that can be filled with whatever we choose. The glass cup simply holds space for whatever it is. The hub is a judgment-free zone and allows our feelings and emotions to be seen. To find your hub, start by getting in a comfortable seated position, connecting with your chair and the floor beneath you. Begin taking slow deep breaths until you feel your body completely relax and give in to the present moment. This is where your hub lies. Explaining the idea of the hub to my teenage clients gave them a sense of calm. They were able to realize that being aware does not require judgment, scientific explanation, or any diagnosis. It was a way for them to step back and just be.

YOU TRY IT!

H.O.M.E Meditation Practice

Meditation can also be used to return to a more desired state, whether that is calm, focused, etc. I have a 4-day beginner meditation practice titled H.O.M.E. Each day, we focus on a letter and complete a 5-minute beginner guided meditation. At the end of each meditation, I provide a daily challenge. These challenges serve to continue the practice throughout your day.

H- Human being. This is your opportunity to be a human. Not striving, no doing, just being.

O- Observing. Simply observing your home (innermost self). Not judging but just being aware.

M- Mend. Opportunity for restoration after neglecting yourself for so long. Pouring back into yourself with loving kindness.

E- Enough. A loving reminder that you are enough and that your home should remind you of that. Recognizing that one can return to this space whenever one needs to.

This beginner practice was curated for the wanderer who wants to connect back with themselves. Providing the opportunity for folks to explore what I title their home. Our innermost self, this quiet subjective inner starting place, usually gets lost in the noise and confusion of stress, oppression, and trauma. Inaccurately viewed as conflict – our true selves are battling to be seen, heard, loved, and felt. No matter what challenges we confront as humanity, we come to our efforts to heal as human beings with a subjective inner life. This subjective inner life is what we will begin to explore. Offering yourself the opportunity to explore this inner world can be a great source of healing. Together we can build a life of resilience-quieting the noise to live freely. To learn more, go to bourneanew.com.

Key Takeaways:

The anger of your Black teen is essentially filling the void of warmth.

- The personal is political, meaning Black male teens' personal lives are constantly influenced by their environment.
- The underlying causes of anger are far more important than the outward behaviors of anger.
- Allowing your teen to partake in some activity that addresses some of the causes of their anger can help them take back their power.
- Meditation can be used as a tool to help them self-regulate.
- Punishing a teen for their emotions can cause more harm and communicate that they should not feel what they are feeling.
- Think of emotions as a car: When such emotion comes up, it should be seen as a signal to pull over and check underneath the hood.
- Think of your teen as a seed. You cannot control what the seed will become. The determining factor in the growth of that seed is how well you take care of its environment. Helping to care for their environment (home, school, community, etc.) will help your teen's growth.
- In the next chapter, we will look at how systems impact your teen's emotions and fuel their anger.

3

Angry Black Man!

"Hence, when we look at the major American institutions relative to African Americans, we observe the following reversals: the economic system keeps them poor; the criminal justice system mediates injustice; the educational establishment creates ignorance and intellectual incompetence; the family institution breeds broken homes and "illegitimate" children; the health and welfare system catalyzes sickness and administers healthcare neglect;... and the religious institutions support the immortality of racial injustice."

Amos N. Wilson, Black-on-Black Violence

We have all heard the saying "angry Black man," but what does this entail? How does such rhetoric hold power? And more importantly, how is it affecting Black male teens? In 1961 James Baldwin, an American author who helped to raise public awareness of racial oppression, was asked by a radio host about being Black in America, and his response was, "To be a negro in this country and to be relatively conscious is to be in a state of rage almost all the time." This statement couldn't be more relevant today.

Our current systems "are designed to deceive, fashioned to seem ameliorative while actually aiding and abetting the injurious exploitation of the population they are supposedly commissioned to help."[2] In other words, the systems in place, labeled as support or relief, encourage harm. They exploit the very people they were designed to help.

To illustrate this point, I will focus on my personal and professional experience with Philadelphia's education system in conjunction with the school-to-prison pipeline. Remember, I was born and raised in Philadelphia, Pennsylvania, and educational practices may look different depending on your state. Even though we will not cover all the systems that may be affecting your teens' anger, they all intersect at some point.

Nelson Mandela said, "education is the most powerful weapon you can use to change the world." After all, this is why you work so hard: hoping that the youth following in your footsteps will have better than you had, including a better education.

When it came to education, my mother did not play. She ensured that I did well in school. She made sure I received high grades and participated in many activities. She hoped that I would have a better life. A life that only education could provide. In part, she was right as:

> *"education is the great engine of personal development.*
> *It is through education that the daughter of a peasant*
> *can become a doctor: that the son of a mine worker*
> *can become the head of the mine; that a child of farm*
> *workers can become the president of a great nation"*
> (Mandela, (1994), Long Walk to Freedom).

---

2. Wilson A. N. (2011). *Black-on-black violence: the psychodynamics of black self-annihilation in service of white domination* (2nd ed.). Afrikan World InfoSystems.

While the value of education holds most of our hopes for a better future, our current educational system may not share that same hope and may have a reversal effect.

If we think back in history to two key moments: Ruby Bridges in 1960 and the start of the industrial revolution, our current struggles within education will make more sense. Ruby Bridges was the first African American to desegregate the all-white William Frantz Elementary school in Louisiana. This courageous and beautiful Black child was crucial in affording Black folks with what we thought would be the same educational opportunities as everyone else. But what if Ruby Bridges never attended William Frantz Elementary? What if we (Black people) never fought to be accepted and included within their (white) system?

This idea that we were able to attend white schools and receive the same education did not equate to equitable or inclusive treatment. Once we were granted access to the system, the assumption was that everyone would now have the same treatment, and it's not true. It is almost as if the abuse and trauma became legal once segregation was illegal. Schools with high Black populations or in poor areas often are shortchanged when it comes to resources and teacher pay. We were misunderstood then and are misunderstood now. The genuine reality is in the research. Black boys are over-identified in special education[3]. They are three times more likely to get suspended or expelled from school than their white student counterparts[4].

According to new research published by the American Psychological Association, "prospective teachers appear more likely to misperceive Black children as angry than white children,

---

3. Halberstadt AG, Cooke AN, Garner PW, Hughes SA, Oertwig D, Neupert SD. Racialized emotion recognition accuracy and anger bias of children's faces. Emotion. 2022 Apr;22(3):403-417. doi: 10.1037/emo0000756. Epub 2020 Jul 2. PMID: 32614194.

4. *Ibid.*

which may undermine the education of Black youth."[5] This anger bias held by teachers can lead to negative experiences at school and often make Black boys feel like "school is just not for me, Mr. Bourne." These negative experiences contribute to the achievement gap. I must add that research highlights white boys' emotions were also hard to judge, but the reality is that people scrutinize white boys less.

Further analysis highlights that misunderstanding, and racial bias puts Black teens at a higher risk of being suspended or expelled. Marian Wright Edelman, the founder and president of the Children Defense Fund, once said, "children are suffering from a toxic cocktail of poverty, illiteracy, racial discrimination, and massive incarceration that sentences poor boys to dead-end and hopeless lives."

Let's analyze one potential life trajectory of this racial bias. I will highlight how it altered one of my clients' lives for years to come. His name was Justin, and he had spent years in prison after being labeled and diagnosed with anger issues. "I felt crazy, Kenn… everyone and everything constantly told me that I had anger issues, and after hearing it enough, it pushed me to accept it." I have heard the phrase "anger issues," casually spoken in conversation regarding Black boys between professionals, and while this may not initially present as an issue, it is dangerous to the future well-being of Black male teens.

Once misunderstood, a Black male is carefully guided through systems of support. This "support" seeks to justify the labeling of having anger issues. This labeling of anger looks different depending on the system one is analyzing, but for my client, his label was diagnosed. For many other clients, they received labels such as intermittent explosive disorder (IED), oppositional defiant disorder (ODD), conduct disorder (CD), and many others.

---

5. *Ibid.*

After being diagnosed in the mental health and medical system, the diagnosis justifies different services labeled as support in the education system. This 'support' for Black male teens often qualifies them for individual education services (IEP). Take Ray, for example, who spent his entire primary education with an IEP, or a friend of mine, now a president and CEO of an organization, who was shoved through many different programs once having an IEP.

To be frank, the only reason they both feel they are successful lies in their ability to consistently believe in themselves and their own abilities, even though their paperwork said something different. With good intentions, the adults around them thought they were helping, but the bar of expectation was set so low that it took years to outwork the label and tap into their full potential.

I use support sparingly because not much changes for the student, but more changes tend to happen for the school (i.e., more money per kid who receives special education services). The school will then claim that it cannot provide the appropriate services that a child needs, resulting in transferring that student, which then interferes with his educational achievement. The consistent pattern of being misunderstood makes it easier for our current systems to justify their placement in juvenile programs.

Juvenile programs are often a "last resort" effort for youth who have not shown any progress, with an arrest or referral to be placed in such a program. Now, they are surrounded by many other Black males whose lives have been commodified to fund an oppressive system, and to no surprise, the student, who was simply misunderstood because no one ever addressed the root causes of his anger, begins to take exhibit behaviors as the other students in the juvenile center. I never understood why our current rules and regulations place all the "bad" kids together but expect a changed behavior.

I forgot to mention that while they go through the many systems, they receive unconscious programming that something is wrong with them. Soon enough, juvenile centers become jails, and jails become prisons. The criminal justice system has not been nice to Black men with a diagnosis. In fact, they shoot or kill them (i.e., Walter Wallace Jr, Miles Hall, Nygill Cullins, etc.). All the while, you are confused about what happened to that sweet boy you raised. And that is how the school-to-prison pipeline happens.

The second critical moment was the industrial revolution. What we know as education today can be linked to the industrial revolution era. This era changed how we worked and were viewed as employees, changing how we were taught. There was a need for factory-level employees who came to work on time to do what they were told and did not think differently. Factory schools[6] were developed in the 19th century, and for the first time, the state provided education. Students were grouped and placed in grades by age and were promoted once they understood the curriculum. Does this sound like our current classroom culture yet or not?

I believe that this also created our toxic work culture that rewards "the good" employees. What was once used to make good factory employees is now used to make good students who are turned into good inmates to work in factories. We have been using antiquated systems that cannot match the current needs of our boys. Therefore, their anger is rooted in systems that have failed them. They have been miseducated by the educational system, criminalized by the criminal justice system, misdiagnosed by the mental health system, and mistreated by the social welfare system.

---

6. https://qz.com/1314814/universal-education-was-first-promoted-by-industrialists-who-wanted-docile-factory-workers/

Okay, so then what? You are probably thinking, "How do I help Black teen males?" One way to help is to understand how they feel and are viewed. Amos Wilson, a Black theoretical psychologist, social theorist, author, and professor of psychology, writes in his book Black-on-Black violence: "to be a sensitive Black male, no matter how innocent, all-American, law-abiding, patriotic, altruistic, and loving is to see the dilated pupils in White women's and old men's eyes, to witness the defensive clutching at pocketbooks, to see yourself reflected in the mirrors of the other's eyes as a mugger, thief, and rapist,"[7] (pg. 35). This demonstrates the idea that we are dangerous and that our anger needs to be controlled.

Anger gets a bad reputation only for Black folks. Everyone gets angry. I would even argue that this emotion was built within us for survival. This can be seen in mistreated kids who become angry when standing up for themselves. Nonetheless, we must teach Black male teens how to process their emotions healthily for a better quality of life and longevity.

In his book, *Between The World And Me*, Ta-Nehisi Coates writes:

> *"But all our phrasing—race relations, racial chasm, racial justice, racial profiling, white privilege, even white supremacy—serves to obscure that racism is a visceral experience, that it dislodges brains, blocks airways, rips muscle, extracts organs, cracks bones, breaks teeth....You must always remember that the sociology, the history, the economics, the graphs, the charts, the regressions all land, with great violence, upon the body."*

---

7. Amos Wilson, The Psychodynamics of Black Self-Annihilation In Service Of White Domination (Afrikan World Infosystems, New York, 1990), pg. 35.

This quote highlights the reality that the body keeps the score. All the -isms are experienced within the body, and we must start learning how to help Black male teens process their reality both healthily and safely. One of the most effective tools I encountered was 'somatic abolitionism' as presented by Resmaa Menakem, a Minneapolis-based therapist, trauma specialist, and author of *My Grandmother's Hands*. He stated that "while we see anger and violence in the streets of our country, the real battle-field is inside our bodies [and] if we are to survive as a country, it is inside our bodies where this conflict needs to be resolved (pg. 22)[8]." The violence and oppression within white supremacy lives within our bodies. Below is a five-step process that I personalized from Resmaa's book, *My Grandmother's Hands*, which can be used as a tool for processing pain and self-regulation.

---

8. Menakem, R. (2017). My grandmother's hands. Central Recovery Press.

YOU TRY IT!

Self-Regulation Activity Practice

One way that I approach this activity is by safely guiding clients through an emotionally painful experience. During this process, I help them calm their rapid, beating hearts and become self-aware using the following technique.

Step 1: Familiarize yourself with your body.

When you have strong feelings and are on the verge of becoming overwhelmed, notice where these urges are coming from. Be quiet and do nothing. Observe these urges without judgment.

Step 2: Stay in the here and now.

In conflict, we tend to mentally leave the present moment and react from our past selves. Reacting from your past self will result in old ways of thinking and old negative habits. To respond with the best parts of you, you must stay present. One way to do this is by noticing the sensation of the wind hitting your face, feeling your clothes touch your body, or referring to your safety plan.

Step 3: Explore the discomfort.

Strong feelings and emotions are sometimes uncomfortable. And when things are uncomfortable, we tend to shy away from them. Instead, explore them by bringing them to your awareness or hub, as mentioned in chapter one, and accept them. Take the strong emotions from step one and explore the discomfort. These emotions are communicating to you. If you run from them, you will miss the opportunity to receive the communication and make the necessary changes. Here are some guiding questions: where do you feel the discomfort the most, and what exactly does this discomfort feel like?

Step 4: Respond vs. React

Once you have completed steps 1-3, you will be able to respond accordingly. Responding is different from reacting. Reacting does not require thought or consideration of others. It is more like a reflex that is embedded within you. Responding requires you to be in a brain state that allows you to logically process and react from a place of care, consideration, and love.

Step 5: Take a hike!

The purpose of step five is to rid yourself of any excess energy you acquired when you were angry. One way to do this is to take a hike, work out, go for a run, walk, etc. You do not have to take a stroll, but that would be my suggestion.

Key Takeaways:

- Our current systems of "support" are encouraging harm.

- Black male teens' anger is rooted in violent systems.

- One way to help process and manage this anger is through the body.

- Anger bias is a real thing and has detrimental effects.

- All the systems (educational, medical, criminal justice, mental health, poverty, nutrition, etc.) intersect. They all impact each other.

- The body is where all the anger and harm get stored. Focusing on the body is key to restoring well-being.

- Carefully consider how systems may be encouraging his anger.

In the next chapter, we will examine anger as a tool for restoring well-being.

I contacted your organization because I have a bright, ambitious 15-year-old son who doesn't want to follow the rules. He spends more time trying to get over the rules than simply abiding by them. I've tried many positive approaches to teach him good decision-making, accepting accountability, etc. He chooses to hang with the wrong crowd and seems like he's doing anything to be "the cool kid." I look forward to hearing from you guys and hopefully getting assistance with my son. Thank you

– Concerned Parent

4

Get Angry and Stay Angry!

Malik was referred to me by another organization that worked with Black males, specifically those intertwined with the criminal justice system. The social worker at the organization received my contact from another therapist who could not take on any new clients. In connecting with the social worker, I learned that the Black male interested in therapy just wanted someone to connect with who looked like him and listened without judgment. I reached out to him, explaining who I was, and to my surprise, he was waiting on my call. The call went as follows:

"...yeah, I like everything you said, Kenn. You sound like you keep it real, and I can relate to you. I especially like the part about trying holistic strategies to help me with my anger."

Anger? What do you mean by anger? Tell me more?

"I don't know what she [the social worker] told you, but I had my dealings with every system, from juvenile detention centers to prison. They told me that I had anger issues, diagnosed me, and had me on medication. But the truth is, I do get upset, but I don't have anger issues. Man, long story short, I think I need help with just navigating some things, but I don't want more medication. That sh*t messes with me, and I don't feel like myself."

During our first call, I was met by a guy with tattoos on his face, short dreadlocks, and a white tank top sitting in his car. Not long into the session, he shared with me what he felt he had been conditioned to think: that anger was wrong and needed some form of treatment. My response to him was, "Get angry and stay angry!"

Now I know that may read as a horrible idea, but strong emotions like anger and fear are warning signals. They signal that something is out of alignment, and that we do not feel safe. These intense emotions communicate that our needs are not being met, we feel unsafe mentally, physically, and racially, and something is not okay.

Let's use our imaginations for a second and imagine a car. When the check engine light blinks or cuts on, it indicates something under the hood needs some attention. It is not yet necessarily a bad or good thing. Only we can determine the degree to which it is a problem after careful consideration. The same goes for anger: it is not necessarily bad or good, and we can only conclude that it is a problem after careful consideration.

When the check engine light comes on, we tend to want it fixed or figure out what is happening. It would be unsafe to continue to drive your car while the check engine light is on. We would never tell the vehicle to stop indicating the check engine light, nor ignore it, hoping it magically cuts off. So why do we expect Black male teens to stop being angry or ignore their anger? Think of anger as the check engine light in your car; to continue getting to your future destinations safely, you must check the engine.

When a person is angry, you should ask what needs are not being met, what he feels, and how you can help address the issue? There could be many answers to the question, and I will only review the three most common unmet needs I have dealt with firsthand: 1) self-esteem/self-acceptance, 2) identity and potential, and 3) lack of love.

Self-esteem and Self-acceptance

Most teens are angrily masking low self-esteem and battling to accept themselves. Aren't we all? But teenagers, mainly because the region of their brains responsible for regulating thoughts, emotions, and actions is not fully developed. In other words, teens function from brain regions responsible for survival, reactivity, experiencing and expressing emotions, detecting threats, and many others.

Through neuroscience and neurobiology, we can understand why they may struggle with their self-esteem. In America, phrases like "be yourself," "self-made," and "get it out the mud" are the perfect ingredients for an individualistic society-one that believes it does not need others. Louis Cozolino writes:

> *"Scientists have had to expand their thinking to grasp the idea that individual neurons or single human brains do not exist in nature. Without mutually stimulating interactions, people and neurons wither and die. In neurons this process is called apoptosis; in humans it is called depression, grief, and suicide. From birth until death, each of us needs others who seek us out, show interest in discovering who we are, and help us feel safe. Thus, understanding the brain requires knowledge of the healthy, living brain embedded within a community of other brains: Relationships are our natural habitat."[9]*

If you take nothing else from this quote, understand that one's self-perception relies on others. In other words, Black male teens may be struggling because we lack community as a people. The African philosophy behind the phrase Ubuntu captures this

---

9. Cozolino, Louis J., author. The Neuroscience of Human Relationships: Attachment and the Developing Social Brain. New York: W.W. Norton & Company, 2014, pg 4.

idea perfectly as it means "I am because we are." Dr. Dan Siegel also highlights this belief within his MWe (Me +We) community gatherings. The idea is that one's belonging and identity is relational.

Modern culture teaches that the self is separate, yet we know that well-being and healing happens in healthy relationships. Therefore, it is not that they are necessarily struggling with self but more that they lack in-group community, culture, and belonging. One that passes down tradition, celebrates their ethnicity, and is connected to its roots. With the invention of race and enslavement, we potentially lost our foundational existence as a thriving community with vibrant cultural traditions at sea. Amos Wilson shares these same sentiments when he states, "For too many African American Youth, being cut off from the paths to legitimate and self-determined personal accomplishment [is] a result of the underdeveloped power of the African American community."[10]

If you are looking for such a community, visit bourneanew. com and join the Anew Community. You can be surrounded by like-minded individuals and participate in live workshops and webinars. You will also have access to many free resources.

Identity and Potential

The need for Black males to achieve power and self-affirmation with no legitimate path can lead to anger. Anger and the expression of anger then becomes an award of achievement in personal identity that otherwise would be unavailable. The violence in our

---

10. Amos Wilson, The Psychodynamics of Black Self-Annihilation In Service Of White Domination (Afrikan World Infosystems, New York, 1990), pg. xix.

communities and violent outward behaviors are ways of expressing frustrations and pent-up anger. Access to violence has not been cut off like the paths to identity and potential. In part, because they are not cut off from access to violent means, violence may be the only way to claim fame in a community that inadequately meets a child's needs and where no social status can be achieved through socioeconomic pathways.[11]

I also want to introduce a swap of the word *purpose* for *potential*. Given that there are whole communities deprived of a sense of purpose, the word purpose can add more stress when asked, "What's your purpose?" I argue that purpose is not something that is found out in the world but realized from within. The idea of potential is strengths-based and offers a less stressful option for one to improve. Black male teens have enormous amounts of potential when they are angry. This spark of motion can be a catalyst for change.

Black males can find identity and regain their power when they recognize that their anger is a compassionate response to experiencing injustice. It is less about explaining or justifying one's anger and more about addressing the root causes through civic action. However, this emotional spark for change is set aside as the focus becomes on punishing the emotion, causing one to feel shame and doubt. Punishing or reprimanding Black male teens' anger can cause them to shrink. It would help if you taught your teen to never shrink due to the comfort levels of others because, unintendedly, you are communicating that their emotions and how they feel come second to others.

---

11. Amos Wilson, The Psychodynamics of Black Self-Annihilation In Service Of White Domination (Afrikan World Infosystems, New York, 1990).

Lack of love

My definition of love comes from the Bible in 1 Corinthians 4-7:

> *"Love is patient and kind. Love is not jealous or boastful or proud or rude. It does not demand its own way. It is not irritable, and it keeps no score of being wronged. It does not rejoice about injustice but rejoices whenever the truth wins out. Love never gives up, never loses faith, is always hopeful, and endures through every circumstance."*[12]

Black male teens are rarely provided this kind of love. History and research have shown that Black male teens are treated and charged as adults. The film, The Central Park Five, depicts the brutal reality of ways Black male teens are found guilty and charged as adults. There have been countless examples of Black male teens being treated differently because of how they are perceived.

Take Michael Brown, a recent high school graduate who was murdered in Ferguson. The cop who killed him reported that he felt like a five-year-old holding onto the hulk. For those who are unfamiliar with the hulk, he is an American comic book character who, when angry, smashes anything in his path. Black teen males are often given adult attributes, non-human strength, and animal-like comparisons.

Keep in mind the African proverb regarding the village being burned down so they can feel the warmth. There is a lack of love that plagues Black male teens. Yes, a mother's love is strong, but it is not enough. They lack love from the community, other Black men, police, and more. We must love one another in a manner that restores well-being. Whether it started during early childhood development, which are the human's foundational

---

12. New Living Translation. YouVersion Bible App, version 9.18.3, LifeChurch.tv 2008

years that shape the rest of their lives, or is a constant reminder when they step outside, the lack of love was a common denominator of all my clients.

I vividly remember how the simple act of hugging the male teens I served in Camden, New Jersey, made a world of difference in building a bond. Consistently telling them I loved them every day was a personal mission of mine, simply because they did not hear it enough. Upon their first time hearing me say it, their response was primarily uncomfortable homophobic slurs telling me that "I am gay" while smiling as if they did not know how to accept my genuine gesture of love.

Beyond the machismo act were sweet boys. Within weeks of constantly showing up, being authentic, and genuinely caring, their response grew from "Kenn, come on with all that gay stuff" to "bring it in" with their arms outstretched. This was their way of saying, "give me a hug." Soon enough, hugs became more regular and derogatory terms regarding showing each other affection became less.

Therefore, teaching, modeling, and expressing love toward Black male teens is essential.

You may be wondering how to do this because the truth is that my race and age may have played a major role in my success. Don't worry. I address how to build successful relationships with Black male teens regardless of race in later chapters. The short easy answer goes back to the rule we learned in elementary school: treat others the way you want to be treated. More importantly, treat others the way they want to be treated! This may read as a simple solution to a complicated problem. Still, simplicity does not decrease value or effectiveness: simply loving on them as they would prefer to be loved is a fundamental principle of human connection. The first step in creating this kind of love is removing self and being present with whoever and whatever is.

A more complicated answer would be to focus more on their strengths and less on their trauma. This means considering their experiences and culture as healing modalities rather than seeing what they have been through as a medical issue. Using anger as an example, below are some questions to help change your perception and help them restore well-being. I phrased them as if you (the parent/caregiver/teacher) are asking the questions:

- What activities are you involved in that you feel are beneficial to your well-being?

- What are some things you do that are rooted in culture and keep you grounded?

- What is something that keeps you going and is unique to you?

To help bring things into perspective, let us pretend your teen likes to skate at the local skatepark. There is a sure way in which skaters build a community that is different from other sports. A question would be, "How does being a skater in your community help you?" This carefully puts your teen at the center while focusing on his strengths to combat his anger. This is the opposite of our current systemic modalities, which is to put the symptoms of his anger at the center and build a treatment plan around the symptoms. I am suggesting that we put the humans back in the center and create a plan around the things that are familiar and healing. This communicates to him that he is more than his anger and, more importantly, that he has the potential to change.

Anger is a great communicator and an indication of unmet needs. Therefore, in an ironic way, urging your teen to stay angry can help them name their emotions and begin creating a change they see fit. Knowing that teens are highly emotional, and their brains are going through numerous transitions, now would be the perfect time to use their emotional spark to create change for themselves and others.

Key Takeaways:

- Think of your teen as a car, and when the check engine light appears (i.e., anger), you must carefully look under the hood (i.e., pass anger) and figure out the root cause.

- Humans were made to exist within the community. We are social creatures in which our self-identity is rooted in others.

- The lack of opportunity for Black men to advance in America affects their ability to accept themselves or embark on a path to becoming their own man.

- A mother's love is not enough, it is helpful, but he also needs safe, unconditional, and forgiving love.

- Anger should be perceived as an unmet need.

- Figure out some things that they are already familiar with to use as strengths for overcoming anger

- Stop shunning certain emotions and rewarding the socially acceptable ones because this communicates that they shouldn't have certain emotions, which can lead to detrimental mental health factors later in life.

- Emotions are uncontrollable, and we have no say as to when they will arise and how they will show up. What we do have control over is how we respond when they do show up. Teaching your teen how to process his emotions safely and carefully respond is a life-saving tool.

In the next chapter, we will analyze how the brain functions concerning anger and how Black male teens can regain control.

5

Your Brain and Anger

"I am reaching out as a concerned Mom of a 15y/r old son. He is having a hard time expressing himself, has become more distant from us and his family, and is struggling academically & socially in High School."

Concerned Parent

The Anatomy of Anger and Biology of the Teenage Brain

Above are common inquiries from concerned parents who want the best for their sons. They seek help, guidance, and a relatable, loving individual qualified to assist their son. You may have read those inquiries and felt I was talking directly about your teen. The reality is that most of them are struggling with the same issues due to drastic brain changes in American adolescents (ages 12-25). Understanding a teenager's brain and important brain regions can help him become the best version of himself. It can help him manage anger, behavior and academic problems, identity and purpose, difficulties fitting in, making good decisions, struggling to make friends, transitioning into adulthood, depression, and anxiety.

Let's look at five important brain regions that may play a vital role in your teen's anger: the brainstem, midbrain, and limbic area, including the hippocampus and amygdala. Remember that I will separate each region for the purposes of explaining, but all areas are connected and work together. Dr. Dan Siegel has a great video on YouTube that illustrates a hand model of the brain. Watching that video will also further an understanding while providing a visual to help paint the picture of what I will discuss in this chapter. I also teach this handy brain model in my workshops at bourneanew.com. The information I provide is best understood within social work, liberal arts, counseling psychology, neuroscience, neurobiology, positive psychology, and interpersonal neurobiology disciplines.

Brain Stem

Our brains are built from the bottom up, like Legos. The brainstem is the first building block of the brain. It connects your brain to your spinal cord. According to Lakeside Global Institute's *Enhancing Trauma Awareness course*, this region is responsible for the following:

- Regulating body temperature
- Breathing
- Blood pressure
- Heart Rate
- Managing Life-sustaining functions
- Reflexive instantaneous functioning: at the most primitive level
- Sensitive to signals of fear, distress, and danger.

If you think about what we need as humans to survive, it makes sense that this region of our brains develops first. If we are honest with ourselves for a second and admit that if it were not for our brain and body performing these essential life functions, we would not remember to do them. As adults, we have become consumed by work that if our bodies did not breathe for us, we would not remember to breathe.

The brainstem and the midbrain (regions we will discuss next) make up the lower brain region, in which lower brain regions are responsible for survival. Dr. Bruce Perry's "The Arousal Continuum, State-Dependent Learning and Response to Threat" chart in his book *The Boy Who Was Raised As A Dog* highlights that if a person is functioning from their brainstem, they may resemble characteristics such as:

- Terror
- Reflexive
- Fainting
- Aggression
- No sense of time[13]

For Black male teens, this can look like but is not limited to blacking out during a fight, uncontrollable terror, anger to the point of destroying things, and a complete loss of control. If they ever get to this point (like I did growing up), it is essential to understand that this brain region is not responsible for intellectual thought or self-reflection. So, asking questions like "What's wrong?" and demanding that they calm down will serve no purpose. They will not be able to comprehend the question or answer you.

One of the main reasons a person can get this low in their brain is a lost sense of safety or if they have been impacted by

---

13. Perry, B. D., & Szalavitz, M. (2007). The boy who was raised as a dog. Basic Books.

trauma, making their brains hypervigilant to events resembling the triggering event. The brainstem is where our fight, flight, freeze, faint, or fawn reactions are. This bottom brain region focuses on keeping you alive, controlling autonomic functions within the body.

An autonomic function such as one's heart rate can provide tremendous insight in predicting one's brain state. There has been a correlation between heart rate and sense of time. For example, a person with a heart rate of 136-160bpm correlates to a loss sense of time implying that this person is functioning from a reflexive state (i.e brainstem). A tip that I tell teachers is to invest in a pulse oximeter and use it as a check-in before class starts, to help give them an idea of the groups pulse.

Another way to help is to prioritize safety and figure out a way to regulate them. A piece of advice that I tell my client's parents is to remove them from the environment immediately they are currently in because something is communicating feelings of unsafety to them. Also, repeating affirming words such as "you are safe" can help them communicate to their brain that they are free to return to themselves, which is a calmer state. Another tool, perhaps the most important, is to mirror calm.

Our brains have mirror neurons, and if these neurons receive a signal of calm, then it will be easier to get a hyper-aroused person to reflect calm. If you are yelling, aroused, and triggered, shouting at and telling your teen to "calm down," it will not be as effective. Therefore, you being calm will also help him calm down. Remaining calm can be difficult as their intense emotions and behaviors can potentially trigger you into acting from a place that is not your best self.

A big part of helping Black male teens is ultimately helping yourself first by finding ways to respond from the best parts of yourself during difficult situations.

Keep in mind that the brainstem is responsible for your autonomic functioning, a way to regulate a person when they exhibit lower brain functioning symptoms is to use these autonomic functions to your advantage. Helping them could look like deep breathing exercises. Some benefits of deep breathing are:

- Slowing down the heart rate
- Aid digestion
- Relieve pain
- Increase immunity function
- Lower blood pressure
- Increase energy
- Restore a sense of calm

Fun fact: The body needs 20-60 minutes to return to its pre-alarmed state, so a goal you could set for yourself is to work your way up to completing deep breathing for at least 20 minutes.

YOU TRY IT!

Deep Breathing Activity Practice

The 4-7-8 breathing technique, developed by Dr. Andrew Weil, is designed to help you control your breathing. He referred to it as the natural tranquilizer for the nervous system. Here is how you practice it:

- Get into a comfortable position. Sitting with your back straight is preferred.

- Place your tongue on the roof of your mouth, behind your top row of teeth.

- Inhale through your nose for 4 seconds.

- Hold your breath for 7 seconds

- Exhale from your mouth for 8 seconds.

- Repeat.

Midbrain

The next region of the brain developed is the midbrain. It sits on top of the brainstem. Lakeside Global Institute's *Enhancing Trauma Awareness course[14] explains that* the midbrain, also called the reptilian brain, is responsible for the following:

- Reactive, not feeling
- Directs impulses throughout the body
- Smell
- Taste
- Swallowing, salivation
- Eye movement, vision, hearing
- Facial sensations
- Vocal sounds
- Respiration
- Controls appetite and sleep
- Maintains equilibrium
- The non-feeling place for conducting self-preserving fight or flight reactions
- The area from which a person operates when in a state of extreme alarm

This region can be easily aroused and overly wired when impacted by trauma. Why is that important? Because located in the mid-brain are dopamine-producing neurons.[15] Dopamine plays

14. Lakeside Global Institute, Enhancing Trauma Awareness, (2006).
15. Poulin JF, Caronia G, Hofer C, Cui Q, Helm B, Ramakrishnan C, Chan

a vital role in the rewarding process, pleasure, and habit learning. The full potential of dopamine is complicated, but for this book, it is essential to note that dopamine is also known as a feel-good hormone. It motivates you to seek the things that will give you a feeling of pleasure.

Remember that midbrain formation happens very early in brain development because these functions are essential for survival. The lower brain regions develop first and are crucial for survival. Dopamine-producing neurons produced in the lower brain states illustrate that it was necessary for our survival and growth. Within three to four weeks of conception, the midbrain starts to form.[16] In context, things like eating and drinking are rewarded with dopamine (rewarding process). Human brains are hardwired to seek out behaviors that release dopamine, which makes sense considering survival's foundational purpose.

Okay, Kenn, what does this have to do with my Black male teen? Adolescence in America has been researched to begin around 12 years old. His brain will begin to undergo drastic changes, in which the dopamine system is also affected. Dopamine is a neurochemical that plays an important role in pleasure and feeling good. Due to the dopamine system going through drastic changes, teens are more susceptible to risk of injury and death. Dr. Dan Siegel highlights adolescent brain changes, which we will discuss later in this chapter. But for now, the key thing to remember is that if brains are hardwired to seek pleasure and feeling behaviors, find ways to provide ample op-

CS, Dombeck DA, Deisseroth K, Awatramani R. Mapping projections of molecularly defined dopamine neuron subtypes using intersectional genetic approaches. Nat Neurosci. 2018 Sep;21(9):1260-1271. doi: 10.1038/s41593-018-0203-4. Epub 2018 Aug 13. PMID: 30104732; PMCID: PMC6342021.
16. Ackerman S. Discovering the Brain. Washington (DC): National Academies Press (US); 1992. 6, The Development and Shaping of the Brain. Available from: https://www.ncbi.nlm.nih.gov/books/NBK234146/

portunity for dopamine to be released healthy and safely. Most notably in a direction that will help him be the man you know he can be.

The Limbic System

Now let's add another block. The limbic area is probably the most crucial area when it comes to your Black male teen. This region is where your teen functions when making decisions and interpreting experiences. Lakeside Global Institute's *Enhancing Trauma Awareness* course explains that the limbic system involves the experience and expression of emotions and contains the amygdala and hippocampus.

It is believed the limbic system is where impulse and emotion live. It is essential to remind you that even though I am compartmentalizing each region, they are connected and work together. So, the limbic system takes its cues from the amygdala, which works with the hippocampus and the lower brain regions (i.e., midbrain and brainstem). Your teenager is functioning from the limbic region and the parts below it.

If you need a refresher, revisit the other brain areas to piece together what areas of the brain Black male teens function within the most. Factor in the impacts of trauma, one may have explosive emotional behaviors and difficulty regulating emotions. For the limbic region to make sense, I must briefly explain the amygdala and the hippocampus in which Lakeside Global Institute's *Enhancing Trauma Awareness*[17] course explains:

---

17. Lakeside Global Institute, Enhancing Trauma Awareness, (2006), pg. 43.

Amygdala:

- Acts as a sentry router.

- All incoming data from the world pass through the amygdala, where decisions are made about whether it goes to the brainstem, midbrain, limbic, or cortex areas based on the storehouse of memories. It determines which part of the brain needs to be activated.

- Works with the hippocampus and other memory banks to decide if, when, and what hormones are released.

- If incoming data create enough emotional charge, the amygdala can hijack the area of the cortex (thinking, reasoning, logic, etc.).

Dr. Bruce Perry believes fear is permanently stored in this region.

Hippocampus[18]:

- Like a computer chip, it stores images and facts so that if something familiar happens, it triggers the memories it has stored.

- Encodes environmental context.

- Transfers information into memory and stores memory.

- The amygdala and hippocampus communicate with each other to determine how the brain should respond in any given situation.

---

18. Lakeside Global Institute, Enhancing Trauma Awareness, (2006), pg. 44

Humans process, store, and retrieve information when necessary.

When he seems to have lost control from something that may seem to be irrelevant, understand that the amygdala may have hijacked his ability to process and make rational decisions due to an overwhelming emotional charge of information. Also, his behavior and actions are rooted in familiar memories to respond accordingly. There is nothing wrong with him, and his behaviors are not irrational, at least not to him. If I were only allowed to give you one piece of advice that could save him, I would tell you that it matters less what you feel or think and more about how he feels. If you can comprehend this idea and understand that what he is exhibiting is from past learned experience, you may be able to help make tremendous progress in his life.

Here is the key, the part of the brain responsible for logical decision-making is not fully developed. Scientists believe the cortex (the thinking part of the brain) is fully developed at 25. That means your teen is functioning from brain regions responsible for survival and emotion. While adult brains use the prefrontal cortex, considered the executive center of the brain, to make rational decisions, an adolescent brain uses the amygdala to interpret emotional expressions. As an adult, you can process emotionally charged situations with logic and ration.

Adult brains have had time to mature and use the prefrontal cortex, the brain's executive center, to make rational decisions. In contrast, teens use the limbic region when interpreting emotional expressions, not by choice but by design. Their actions are guided more by the emotional and reactive amygdala and less by the thoughtful, logical frontal cortex. Research has also shown that exposure to drugs and alcohol during the teen years can change or delay these developments. Based on the stage of their brain development, adolescents are more likely to:

- Act on impulse
- Misread or misinterpret social cues and emotions
- Get into accidents of all kinds
- Be involved in fights
- Engage in dangerous or risky behavior

Adolescents are less likely to:

- Think before they act
- Pause to consider the consequences of their actions
- Change their dangerous or inappropriate behaviors

These brain differences don't mean that teens can't make good decisions or tell the difference between right and wrong. It also doesn't mean they shouldn't be held responsible for their actions. However, an awareness of these differences can help parents, teachers, advocates, and policymakers understand, anticipate, and manage the behavior of adolescents.

Dr. Daniel Siegel created the acronym ESSENCE as the basis for well-being both during this crucial period of growth and change, as well as throughout the lifespan:

The Essence of Adolescence[19]		
ES	Emotional Spark	**Highly active processing of emotion that influences cortical reasoning** •Downside: Moodiness, irritability, sensitive, emotional states •Upside: Passion and energy
SE	Social Engagement	**Driven towards peers and away from parents** •Downside: Risk of sacrificing personal values in exchange for peer acceptance; total exclusion of adults •Upside: Supportive relationships and development of lifelong relationship skills
N	Novelty	**Changes in the dopamine (reward) and limbic (evaluative) systems of the brain** •Downside: Risk of injury and death highest during this time •Upside: Courage to explore and leave the familiar and certainty of the home and enter the larger world
CE	Creative Exploration	**Mental pushing away from the "status quo;" new perspectives and ways of thinking** •Downside: Potential to feel out of place, disoriented •Upside: Innovations, creativity, and the ability to adapt

19. *Mindsight Institute.* (2019). Mindsightinstitute.com. https://www.mindsightinstitute.com/

This ESSENCE framework provides the information necessary to help navigate this critical developmental period. Understanding his brain development will better equip you to assist him where he needs, ultimately saving Black male teens.

Key Takeaways:

- It doesn't matter what you think or feel as the adult but how they feel as a teen. If you can grasp this, you will be able to have a deeper connection with your Black male teen.

- Teens are very emotional (to no surprise), which can also be used to their advantage if they learn how to manage them.

- Teens are responding from very low brain states (i.e., brainstem, midbrain, and limbic) and not higher brain states responsible for logical decision making.

- Our brains are built to seek pleasure and rewarding behaviors, which can be tricky for an emotional teen. Knowing this, try to provide ample opportunity for safe activities that will have the same effect.

- Due to the drastic brain changes during adolescence, your teen is vulnerable to dysregulation. Helping them regulate is critical.

In the next chapter, we will discuss anger within the body as our bodies hold a form of knowledge different from our brains.

6

How Does Anger Show Up In Your Body?

Vagus Nerve

Our bodies have a different way of communicating our emotions than our brains. Although it is different, it is very effective once we become aware of how to listen to our bodies. Our bodies were built to house our souls and sustain us. In that respect, if something signals harm to either of these aspects, our bodies will signal that something is not right. By not right, I mean both uncomfortable and disconnected from within.

It is essential to understand that everything is connected. Your brain communicates to your body, and your body transmits to your brain. Both your brain and body take in information from people and the environment. Energy and information are received, processed, stored, and referenced when needed. I say all that to preface how anger resides in the body.

Author Resmaa states, "New advances in psychobiology reveal that our deepest emotions—love, fear, anger, dread, grief, sorrow, disgust, and hope—involve the activation of our bodily structures. These structures—a complex system of nerves—connect the brainstem, pharynx, heart, lungs, stomach, gut, and spine."[20] The complex system of nerves that Resmaa is referring

---

20. Menakem, R. (2017). *My grandmother's hands*. Central Recovery Press. Pg. 29

to is the vagus nerve. More specifically, the vagus nerve is the longest cranial nerve, which is why it is also known as the wandering nerve. It runs from our brainstem through our lungs, heart, liver, spleen, stomach, pancreas, gallbladder, kidney, and large and small intestines[21]. This wandering nerve is also called the mind-body connection. The vagus nerve influences our[22]:

- Breathing
- Swallowing
- Heart rate
- Blood pressure
- Mood
- Mucus salivation
- Skin and muscle sensations
- Speech circulation
- Digestion
- Gut health
- Bladder movements
- Orgasms
- Fertility

Resmaa refers to the vagus nerve as our soul nerve because it essentially is the "unifying organ of the entire nervous system."[23] The vagus nerve is the central part of our parasympathetic nervous system. The parasympathetic nervous system is part of our body's autonomic nervous system and helps the body to

21. Menakem, R. (2017). *My grandmother's hands*. Central Recovery Press.
22. *Ibid.*
23. Menakem, R. (2017). *My grandmother's hands*. Central Recovery Press. Pg. 258

relax, aid digestion, etc. The function of the vagus nerve can become impaired by stress, anxiety, poor lifestyle, smoking, drinking alcohol, overworking, lack of exercise, unhealthy eating, and sleep.

When it cannot perform to the best of its abilities (agitated), we are susceptible to diseases (dis-ease) such as depression, obesity, anxiety, cardiovascular disorder, diabetes, digestive disorders, chronic inflammation, kidney malfunction, infertility, and even Parkinson's.

Here are some natural ways to soothe our vagus nerve:

- Breathing
- Mediation
- Exercise
- Singing and chanting
- Massages hugging
- Yoga
- Laughing
- Healthy diet

You can use breathing exercises to practice controlling your breathing, resulting in the ability to drastically affect your nervous system. A slow deep-breathing practice helps to manage heart rate and communicates to the vagus nerve. The vagus nerve then gathers signals from multiple places in the body and realizes that things must be calm and restful. The vagus nerve then passes this message to the brain (brainstem). So, the vagus nerve receives and sends signals throughout our body and to our brainstem. Remember, the brainstem develops first and is responsible for our autonomic responses. When you nurture the vagus nerve, love, empathy, connectedness, intuition, and well-being become possible.

For this book, the vagus nerve plays a role in our mood. Being the central part of our parasympathetic nervous system, which helps regulate our stress responses, inherently affecting our mood. Also, the vagus nerve lengths down to our gut and play a role in affecting one's mood. In furthering our understanding of the mind-body connection, scientists believe that we have more than one brain, in which the gut serves as our second brain due to how much they interact. For example, just the thought of eating can release stomach juices[24]. An even better example would be the idea of feeling like you need to use the restroom when you are nervous or feeling butterflies in your stomach from certain situations.

Our gut is sensitive to intense emotions like anger, fear, sadness, anxiety, depression, etc. Our brains and guts communicate. Stomach issues can affect our mood as the signals from an irritable stomach communicate with our brain. Harvard medical school states, "a person's stomach or intestinal distress can be the cause or the product of anxiety, stress, or depression."[25] Our gut holds the second most intricate set of neurons outside of our brains, in which scientists have found that gut bacteria can produce neurotransmitters such as dopamine (the feel-good hormone). As stated earlier, dopamine plays a crucial role in our mood.

You may be telling yourself right now, "Okay, Kenn, don't get too nerdy on me," and "how does this information help me?"

Understanding the mind-body connection and its relation to emotions, like anger, can help him to thrive holistically and not rely on other methods that contain suicide warning labels

24. https://www.health.harvard.edu/diseases-and-conditions/the-gut-brain-connection
25. *Ibid.*

(i.e., psychotropics). I cannot stress the importance of healthy eating, exercising, meditation, spending time in nature, etc. Most of the time, these activities are mentioned solely with our mental health, but this is bigger than mental health- this is how you restore well-being.

The truth is that the medical industry knows the importance of the vagus nerve and how it helps with things like depression. A surgical practice called Vagus Nerve Stimulation (VNS) was developed for those who are treatment-resistant (do not respond to psychotropics)[26]. A pacemaker-like device attached to a stimulating wire threaded along the vagus nerve is implanted in the body. This FDA-approved practice has been a treatment modality since 2005 to treat severe cases of depression.[27]

As a passionate advocate for holistic modalities due to the dark history of medical experimentation on Black Americans, I focus on natural ways to help one manage their symptoms, ultimately restoring well-being. Harriet A. Washington has a book called *Medical Apartheid* if you want to learn about Black Americans' untrust in the medical system.

The reality is that there are things that we have been doing as people that stimulate our vagus nerve (i.e., humming and tapping.) Have you ever caught yourself humming a song? I always tapped on desks and made beats on anything I could get my hands on. I also could hum a song's tune well enough that my classmates could guess the song. To my surprise, I have been unconsciously soothing myself for years while simultaneously getting in trouble for it (i.e., kicked out of class).

---

26. O'Reardon JP, Cristancho P, Peshek AD. Vagus Nerve Stimulation (VNS) and Treatment of Depression: To the Brainstem and Beyond. Psychiatry (Edgmont). 2006 May;3(5):54-63. PMID: 21103178; PMCID: PMC2990624.
27. *Ibid.*

Imagine if teachers knew this information and how it could be applied to help regulate students. I would not have been kicked out of class as much or suspended. Instead, it would have been a perfect time to check in to see how I was doing. In addition, there is a rapper named Kid Cudi, who is notoriously known for his signature humming within his songs. I now understand why so many folks love it- it's soothing. I am not sure if they realize it, but when they hum, they are soothing their vagus nerve, which sends calming signals to other areas in their body.

I would even go a step further and correlate rapper Kid Cudi's hum resembles the 'OM' chant in Buddhist culture, in which the benefits of chanting "OM" has been studied, confirmed.[28]

Another vital aspect much quieter than humming or tapping is how we communicate with ourselves. Communication with ourselves typically starts as a thought that leads to perceptions and beliefs, resulting in a behavior. In therapy, they treat this with a process called Cognitive Behavioral Therapy (CBT). Picture a triangle and at the top point of the triangle reads thoughts, the second point reads behaviors, and the last end says feelings. In simpler terms, how our thoughts ultimately determine our behaviors and feelings, and the cycle repeats. With CBT, a therapist would work with you to figure out why you are having specific thoughts, where they stem from, and how to replace them with healthier options, ultimately restoring well-being.

This framework is essential to comprehend because researchers from Queen's University in Canada discovered that the average person has 6,000 thoughts per day[29]. If this is true, how

28. Kalyani BG, Venkatasubramanian G, Arasappa R, Rao NP, Kalmady SV, Behere RV, Rao H, Vasudev MK, Gangadhar BN. Neurohemodynamic correlates of 'OM' chanting: A pilot functional magnetic resonance imaging study. Int J Yoga. 2011 Jan;4(1):3-6. doi: 10.4103/0973-6131.78171. PMID: 21654968; PMCID: PMC3099099.
29. https://www.queensu.ca/gazette/stories/discovery-thought-worms-opens-window-mind

many of us think the same thing repeatedly, finding ourselves lost in thought?

In neuroscience, the idea of "neurons that fire together wire together" is synonymous with CBT. So, when we do something repeatedly, the brain will trigger the same neurons each time. This act helps us become better at things as we learn, store, and recall information. The more we experience an event, the more substantial the connection becomes. The issue becomes when we constantly think negatively about ourselves. We are strengthening the relationship in our brains to the point where a simple thought can automatically make us feel a certain way without realizing it. So, let's take the time to explore this idea of negative self-talk and the power of words.

Disciplines such as positive psychology use an asset-based approach that focuses on nurturing a person's strengths instead of their shortcomings. This approach is similar to the one I use: a salutogenic approach that focuses on restoring well-being and health. One way to help nurture from within is to monitor how one thinks and communicates with self. The most used practice regarding positive-self talk is affirmations, which are positive short phrases that support one's mental and emotional well-being. I typically personalized affirmations depending on the goal of my clients.

For example, one of my clients struggled to grow because of his past mistakes. He felt like his ability to move on was stunted because he could not let go of his past. So, for this client, an example of a few affirmations that I assigned for him to write down on sticky notes and stick onto places that he frequently visited (i.e., bathroom mirror, refrigerator door, computer screen, etc.):

1. I am not my mistakes.
2. I forgive myself for the mistakes I made when I did not know any better.
3. I release all shame and guilt from my past and choose to live in the present.

These affirmations helped him challenge his negative thoughts about himself and offer a new way of thinking.

Inner Exploration of Emotions Within The Body

I would be doing you a disservice if I did not go deeper into the power of words concerning our brains and bodies, emotions, and the potential effect that lies within the words we speak to ourselves and others. This section gives you a basic understanding of what may be happening internally, so you can feel more equipped to change what's happening externally. In other words, as the great Maya Angelou once said, "When you know better, you do better."

The idea of emotions lives within the limbic area of our brains. The limbic area is responsible for how we experience and express emotions and motivation and determines whether things are good or bad. Anger can internalize itself as low self-esteem. Low self-esteem usually presents as some emotion that grows from our perception of something being bad or not good enough, resulting in low motivation.

It is essential to add that within the limbic area exist the amygdala and hippocampus. As a quick refresher, the amygdala acts as a router, constantly scanning the world and determining where that information goes (i.e., to other parts of the brain). It can hijack the part of your brain responsible for making logical decisions if incoming data creates enough emotional charge. In this case, the person will react out of pure emotion or survival. The hippocampus stores images and facts so that if something familiar happens, it triggers the memories it has stored. The amygdala and hippocampus communicate with each other to determine how the brain should respond in any given situation.

For example, let's say your teenager was cheated on in a past relationship. Their amygdala receives this emotionally charged event as behaviors, words, smells, etc., and their hippocampus stores these as facts. They will begin to internalize this situation and replay it over and over in their head, to the point where they somehow find a way to blame themself as the cause of their ex's actions. Feelings of embarrassment, hurt, shame, guilt, etc. take-over, and now their body has embedded a reaction to intimate relationships.

It is important to note that everything I just described happens at lightning speed. Keeping in mind that the amygdala is where fear, learned from past experiences, is permanently stored, fast forward to their next or current relationship where they are hyper-vigilant to similar words and behaviors from their past. Once they (body and brain) perceive any resemblance of their past relationship, whether through words, behaviors, etc., their brain will do what it was designed to do and ensure that they do not feel this pain again. These similar behaviors from their partner will trigger their amygdala and hippocampus to perceive this current situation as the last painful relationship, automatically triggering feelings of embarrassment, hurt, shame, guilt, etc. They become emotionally reactive to their partner because they perceive things are going downhill.

Meanwhile, a simple conversation could have occurred to fact-check their perceptions. They did not choose to converse with their partner because whenever they first experienced that situation (i.e., break up), their brain and body embedded a response. Whatever that response was is how they show up in every similar case unless they actively work at rewiring this embedded response. An effective way to rewire the brain is through affirmations. They can help rewire new thoughts to help them live in the present and not the past.

Lastly, I must touch on the power of words. Have you ever heard the saying, "sticks and stones may break my bones, but words won't hurt me?" Well, that's not true, and words are more powerful than we once knew. Before I briefly explain the potential power of words, please keep an open mind and heart, as what I am hypothesizing may be a stretch.

When I would ask my clients, "have you ever heard of affirmations" or "speaking kindly to yourself," the answer was often no. To give you some context regarding the power of words, I will touch on Suzette Haden Elgin's book, *You Can't Say That To Me.*

Suzette Haden Elgin was an American researcher in experimental linguistics, construction and evolution of languages, and poetry and science fiction writer. In her book, *You Can't Say That To Me*[30], she provides a critical framework and an 8-step program on how to deal with verbal abuse. The book does not directly use the word affirmations or discuss how one should speak to oneself. Instead, it analyzes the communication that we have with each other.

However, it does mention some things about the power of words, and I hypothesize that regardless of who you are talking to, whether it's yourself or someone else, the words that we choose to speak hold power. Most of this power lies in our perception of how we perceive the words to be true or not true. All perceptions are magical lies, also known as illusions, in which illusions are mistaken for reality until we understand the trick behind them.

---

30. https://archive.org/details/youcantsaythatto00elgi/page/n7/mode/2up

Below are some powerful quotes that I pulled from her book that will help you rethink words and how we currently use them[31]:

> *"Verbal abuse is literally dangerous to your health and safety and well-being. Nothing you can do is more likely to change your life dramatically for the better than getting rid of verbal abuse in your own language environment," (preface, pg. v). The tongue has the power of life and death (Proverbs 18:21*

> *And the most powerful stimulus for changing a person's mind is not a chemical. It's not a shock. It's not a baseball bat. It's a word." (G. Miller, quoted in "giving Away Psychology in the 80s," in Hall 1980, p. 41).*

> *In a person whose basic response to any situation is hostility, suspicion and a desire for control, stress hormones constantly surge through the body because everything is perceived as a threat." ("How Hostile Thinking Makes You Heart-Sick," 1989, p.5)*

The lesson from Elgin's book is about the power of words and the real effects that it has on our well-being. You can read her book online for free at https://archive.org/details/youcantsaythatto00elgi[32].

Keep this idea in your mind as you read this book. Your life can significantly be happier and healthier with daily practice in stopping your overwhelming negative thoughts and replacing them with affirmations. If you would like more help, I created a guide designed to help remind you of all that you know you are. It was designed to shine a light on that dark part within your soul where your true self hides. It is a free PDF download at www.bournenanew.com.

---

31. *Ibid*
32. https://archive.org/details/youcantsaythatto00elgi

Key Takeaways:

- Even though we may not see it, our words hold power. We can either speak life into ourselves or sickness.

- The vagus nerve (aka soul nerve) is vital in understanding the mind-body connection. It communicates to many other areas within our body that we are either distressed or need to calm down.

- There are holistic ways to help soothe the vagus nerve, such as meditation and deep breathing, which will help manage your emotions.

- Our bodies communicate differently than our brains, yet they are interconnected as they communicate with each other.

- Our gut houses our deep emotions, such as fear, anger, grief, and love.

- Eating healthier foods can also improve your mood.

- Talking to yourself with loving kindness can positively affect your emotions.

- Learning your body's form of communication will help you overcome anger.

- Affirmations are a tool to weaken the connection between their negative thoughts and anger. There is no right or wrong way when developing an affirmation. The only important piece is that it speaks deeply to the soul.

In the next chapter, we will discuss six techniques for managing, reframing, and redirecting your Black male teen's anger.

7

G.R.O.U.N.D

Six Techniques For Managing, Reframing, And Redirecting Your Anger

When working with teens, the number one question is: "What are some tools and practices I can use to manage my anger?" This question implies that they are looking for ways to manage and cope. They are not just looking for any tool but one that speaks to them and their culture. A tool or strategy that understands their lived experiences and considers their racial identity. They want something that will allow them to take their power back. Most of our systems of support in America seek to make us less miserable.

Here, Black teen boys are looking to be happy. Black boys want to exist as they truly are. As a society, we have done everything to go against this simple reality. Instead of addressing the systems affecting them, we address the symptoms leaving them to feel that something is inherently wrong with them for having an emotion. My goal is not just to provide you with strategies to help your Black male teen cope but to help them find the meaning within themselves to move in a health-promoting direction. This 6-step technique will introduce coping skills such as practicing mindfulness to manage emotions better.

In this chapter, you will learn an acronym that may help Black male teens manage their anger and become self-aware. This technique is best practiced with sticky notes around the house, like posters or pictures, as a constant reminder that they are in control. The acronym GROUND helps tame the beast.

G: Get moving.

The benefits of exercise for mental health have been established and are evident in the research. Exercise and movement help reduce anxiety, depression, and negative moods, improving self-esteem and more. I use the G in GROUND a lot. I typically will go for a run or workout. Knowing that exercise does wonders for my body and brain, I now use it in place of anger outbursts. It helps me clear my mind and release the burst of energy I feel when I am angry. I must preface the rest of this section by recognizing that it took much practice to become a replacement behavior, and if your teen does not see the benefit of exercise, you may need to do some convincing prior to simply suggesting exercise.

For Black male teens to truly appreciate moving and the importance of it, it is imperative that I provide you both with a framework or pathway that is both practical and safe. The pre-requisite for G in the acronym GROUND is what I call the five anchors. I personalized these steps that Resmaa Menakem created initially to manage conflict. Since Black male teen anger is interpreted as conflict, it is appropriate that we discuss these steps before moving on.

YOU TRY IT!

Five Anchor Activity Practice

When in conflict or feeling overwhelmed, do this practice in order from one to five. Once reaching step five, you will see that it resembles the G in GROUND.

1. **Settle your body - JUST BREATHE**
   a. Stay quiet. Refrain from the urge to respond/ react immediately. Letting go of the notion of constantly feeling like you have to say or do something because we think saying or doing something is the same as standing up for ourselves. JUST BREATHE.

2. **Staying Present - OBSERVE WITH KINDNESS**
   a. Simply notice any sensations in your body during the conflict.
   b. Try to feel what it's like to have your clothes touch your skin, the wind hitting your face, etc.
   c. Remove the tongue from the roof of the mouth.

3. **Analyze Discomfort - ACCEPTANCE**
   a. Accept the discomfort.

   b. Do not ignore or judge.

   c. Do not distract yourself or run away from the uncomfortable.

   d. Stick with it long enough and notice when it passes.

4. Respond - WITH EASE
   a. Slowly feel your way back into the situation, conflict, etc.

   b. Don't try to predict what will happen next

   c. When you start to think how much this situation urges strong emotion, bring yourself back to your body

   d. Safely ease back into the conflict and respond from the best parts of yourself

5. Shake it off
   a. Safely eliminate any energy left (i.e., workout, run, etc.)

   b. Partake in a physical activity that allows you to expel any negative energy left from the situation

   c. Your body needs 20-50 minutes to return to its pre-alarmed state

Adopted from *My Grandmother's Hands: Racialized Trauma and Pathway To Mending Our Hearts and Bodies*

Now, in continuation of the GROUND acronym, on to the R.

R: Record and Reflect.

Record and reflect looks like keeping a log or a journal of some sort – one that tracts your mood and the other factors that contribute to your moods, such as food, movement, and sleep. When working with clients, our check-ins would consistently consist of me inquiring about their mood, what they are eating, and how they are sleeping. I always inquire about these other aspects because so much of managing anger involves other areas in our lives.

Remembering that it's all connected, we should consider all of it when trying to understand the anger. For example, if our brain communicates with multiple organs within our body, these organs receive signals from people, places, and environments. We should analyze it all when learning to manage our emotions. Here is a simple framework that may help you and your Black male teen with managing their emotions, specifically anger:

When anger is present:

- **People**: Who was around and involved?
- **Environment**: What physical space were you in?
- **Food**: What food did you eat before or during the event?
- **Energy**: What was your energy before and after you were angry
- **Bodily Sensations**: What do you remember feeling when you were angry (i.e., heart beating fast, blood rushing, headache, etc.)

Jotting down some quick notes after every time you are angry can begin to help you recognize your triggers and how to manage them. If this is hard to do, that most likely means you are still mad and not in your thinking brain, even though you may appear to be. If this is you, then practice these recentering techniques to regain a sense of calm.

YOU TRY IT!

Recentering Activity Practice

Find a space where you can safely exist. Somewhere quiet would be preferred. If that's not possible, right where you are is okay too.

Sit comfortably. Feel your butt connecting with the surface of whatever you're sitting on, recognizing the surface you are sitting on is connected to the earth.

Begin inhaling through your nose and filling up with oxygen. Hold. Then exhale slowly out of your mouth.

Repeat this breathing exercise. Every time you think about the overwhelming experience, say to yourself, "breathing" to help bring your awareness back to your breath.

Repeat this until you feel like you have arrived.

You must realize the power of your mind and its ability to perceive. Here is the key: compare your perception with reality, and if those two things are not aligned, you must reconsider why you are angry. In other words, our perception is subjective, leaving reality objective. Our perception can be triggering, causing a long list of reactions that can be avoided. Writing and reflecting on what happened is excellent practice in learning to compare your perspective with reality.

Recording and reflecting on your emotions is a significant first step in managing your anger because you cannot get a different outcome from a behavior/emotion you don't know.

O: Open your airways.

The **O** within the GROUND acronym focuses on breathing and its importance in managing emotions. We must realize that our body has been sustaining us all this time as it reminds us to breathe. How many times do you tell yourself to "breathe?" If it weren't for our bodies breathing for us, then we would not do it. We have become too busy with the things of the world that we often neglect ourselves. I am not referring to the simple act of breathing here. I am referring to the power and transformation within our breath when we combine it with present practices like meditation. Dan Siegel's book *Aware* mentions how we can train our awareness. Early in the book, he provides imagery regarding our consciousness and how we can teach it to our benefit. Practicing how to "increase the mind's capacity for being aware so that you will be able to adjust the ratio of the experience of awareness itself." He calls this "cultivating consciousness," which means training your mind. Within the invitation of his book, he writes:

> *"There is an old saying that consciousness is like a container of water. If you take a tablespoon of salt and place it in a small container, say, the size of an espresso cup, the water will certainly be too salty to drink. But if your container is much larger– say it can hold many gallons of water–the same tablespoon of salt, now placed into this vast amount of liquid, will taste fresh. Same water, same salt; simply a different ratio, and the drinking experience is different."*

This analogy allows us to understand our awareness and consciousness and how we can train our minds. The container of water represents your consciousness, and the salt represents whatever you are aware of at that moment. For this book, salt represents anger. When our containers of water (i.e., consciousness) are small, then life's issues seem overwhelming. For example, growing up in southwest Philly made it very difficult for me to expand my container of consciousness. My environment of drugs, violence, guns, low income, etc., significantly impacted my ability to change my perspective. Things like causing physical harm to others who I felt disrespected me seemed as if this was normal.

Living in this oppressive systemic environment shaped my perception of the world, causing my perception to be skewed. This skewed perception made the water in my container extremely salty, prohibiting my ability to taste the freshness of life and free my perspective. Therefore, a place to begin when trying to help your Black male teen manage their anger is encouraging them to work on their breath. A simple 4-second inhale through the nose while expanding one's belly, and a 7-second exhale from the mouth can help control one's anger. Practicing slowing down their breath will help to combat the reflexive behaviors that they exude when angry.

U: Use diversions!

There is a saying in neuroscience, "neurons that fire together, wire together." In other words, every thought, feeling, and experience triggers neurons in your brain, which form networks. When you repeat an experience, thought, or feeling over and over, your brain learns to trigger that same response-eventually allowing for that response to become automatic or reflexive. This idea is important because it implies that if we consistently repeat something, let's say mindfulness, the neuronal network connections become stronger.

This concept is also two-fold because what is happening with our Black male teens is that their neuronal network connection with anger is being used so often that it becomes a part of their identity. Due to the strength of the connections they have formed within their brains, their brains react and respond to situations the same every time. To be fair, this is not something most people are aware of, and I genuinely do not believe any one person intends to do this, but things like one's environment, culture, neighborhood, etc., play a vital role in what neurons are fired and wired. It is essential to teach your Black male teen this concept because understanding this concept could help them create a new response or reaction-one that is healthy and safe.

Picture this: it is your first time in the gym. Your goal is to tighten up the loose, flabby skin under your upper arm. You then pick up a 50-pound weight and cannot lift it. So, you then grab the 10-pound weight and realize that this is much easier for you to manage. After consistently going to the gym, you work your way up to the 50-pound weights you could not lift before. Apply this same analogy to managing emotions.

It won't be easy when your teen first begins practicing mindfulness to help combat anger and adopt a new response to life's challenges. It is vital to recognize that your first time practicing such a technique will not provide any results. His ability to work through his anger and replace the negative associated behaviors needs to be exercised more. His anger and negative behaviors have been practiced so much that he associates his identity with them.

The key is consistent practice. He has to re-train his mind and rewire brain connections. It would be misleading if I did not prepare you by saying this may be an uncomfortable experience due to the novelty of it all, but just because things are uncomfortable does not mean they are bad. His brain will want to use what it has been using to respond to situations such as anger, so he will be competing with his own mind at this point.

The first step in managing behavior is to "stop doing." Resist the urge to do, say, or act when feeling overwhelmed. Just stop. Practicing stopping, as if you are playing freeze tag, will help him regain control of his behaviors. Eventually, he can divert his attention to something positive instead of the event overwhelming him to the point of anger.

N: Nourish, restore, and rest.

Remember, what you put in is what you give out, so if you nourish your body and mind in healthy ways, your behaviors will illustrate that same thing.

An example of this would be to examine how you are currently feeding your brain and body. This does not only consider food but also how we feed our minds. This includes music, television, streaming, podcasts, social media, our friend groups, etc. Remember, everything is connected, so feeding your mind is the same as feeding your body and vice versa. If your Black male teen constantly listens to music that mentions drugs, killing, violence, etc., then do not be surprised when his behaviors resemble a music video. This goes along with the saying *the grass is not greener on the other side but where you water it*. So, what are you watering? That is what will grow.

If he has a trusting friend group, this can bring restoration into his life. Healthy relationships allow us to work through our triggers safely. Having someone to open up to and talk about things that are stressing you out to someone who won't judge you may feel like a weight has been lifted. Confiding in those you trust to hold the stress with you can make the stress less heavy to carry on your own.

Lastly, rest is vital to managing just about everything in life. Rest is different from sleep. Have you ever felt tired after a night's sleep? Rest involves your whole being. Some cultures take rest very seriously. Rest can take many forms: emotional rest, physical rest, social rest, etc. However, they are different from what you may think. Each form of rest requires an exploration of your whole being. Emotional rest may require you to examine the things that drain you or explore the emotions you neglect through a reflective practice like meditation. Regardless of what type of rest it may be, the important idea to understand is that making time for rest can have a positive effect on managing emotions.

D: Decompress.

Give yourself space and time to feel your emotions; they are valuable.

The body takes 20 to 60 minutes to return to its pre-alarmed state. Refer to your safety plan in Chapter One to help guide how to spend your alone time. This is the number one thing I tell my clients in my therapeutic coaching program: take time for yourself; as Black men in America, we have been socialized to care for everyone but ourselves, and creating time for ourselves can make a world of difference.

Black boys feel as if they are not nurtured or groomed in ways that safely allow them to express their emotions, so they have difficulty communicating and expressing themselves. The reality is that at some point, we must do it ourselves, but most of us need help knowing where to start. Start by carving out five minutes of the day that is solely spent with yourself. Whether you are doing nothing or enjoying an activity, this time should be spent just being. It may help to have a safe space to do this, like a room in the house or a section in a park where you can chill.

When he becomes angry, remind him of this acronym. Place each letter in commonly used spots in your home so that he is reminded of them often because the more he uses these techniques, the stronger he becomes in managing his anger.

Key Takeaways:

- Movement improves mood. Stretching, exercising, working out, going for a walk, etc., have benefits that go beyond appearance.

- Track your emotions and the correlations between your emotions and what is happening at that moment.

- GROUND-ing yourself requires a deep commitment to understanding who you are as a person.

- The overall goal is to become comfortable with the uncomfortable process of navigating life's challenges.

- Place each letter as a poster around the house as a reminder. Have him add this acronym to the safety plan he made in Chapter One.

8

Releasing Anger in a Positive Way

A s I slowly rolled over to grab my phone and see what time it was, I had a text message that said, "Are you awake?" I rubbed my eyes to get a better look at who it was from. I then noticed that I had a missed call, too. My best friend and I have a close bond, so I know when something is up depending on how the text is typed.

"Shit," I said as I sat up quickly. *"Something is up!"*

So, I quickly grabbed my phone and called them.

"Did I wake you?" they stated. *"Sorry if I disturbed you...."*

"No, what's up," I said.

"So, they killed him... and I am on my way to tell the family. But I wanted to check in with you to see if there is a better way I can say this," they explained.

"Wait, what? Killed who? When did this happen?" I asked. My heart was pounding. My head was ringing, and that's how my morning started.

"Check your phone. It's all over the news. I sent you the videos that they sent me," they finished.

Life as a Black boy is no different than life as a Black man. You are trapped in an hourglass of never-ending sand. It's like you can see the outside world and the things happening in it, but somehow you are stuck in a different reality. A reality that is always grieving. Grieving loved ones, friends, ways of living, change, the unknown, and life. Constantly wondering what it would have been like if we, as a people, had the opportunity and access to power, resources, and financial security. What would life be like? Dreaming of all the culture, language, and community buried at the bottom of oceans. What would life be like if violence and murder did not exist? Is there any place that I can go and simply be myself?

As Black men, we are socialized to be hypervigilant-repeatedly looking over our shoulders. Is this what it's like to be human? To wake up with fast-paced heart rates, headaches, and tight chest? Does everyone start their day like this? How do I carry on with my day navigating grief, sadness, and heaviness? I feel for my ancestors and present-day family. I want to be able to think clearly sometime. It was summarized best by a client seeking holistic coaching. "I really just don't want to be angry anymore." We have concluded that our anger is something that we need to rid ourselves of and not have.

Teens often turn to unhealthy ways to cope with their anger. This is structural and by design. Peter Levine and Maggie Kline talk about symptoms of trauma during adolescence in their book *Trauma Through A Child's Eyes*. They explain how normal teen development is a chaotic period due to hormonal changes, inhabiting a new body, and transitioning to adulthood. One of the most prominent points that they make is "adolescent symptoms still resemble those of adults.[33]"

That statement is very important, especially for the purpose of this book, because it highlights the impact of adolescence on adulthood, meaning that if we can address some of these symptoms and challenges during adolescence, we may see healthier

33. Levine P. A. & Kline M. (2019). Trauma through a child's eyes: awakening the ordinary miracle of healing. North Atlantic Books.

functioning adults. Some key takeaways from this section of their book are the signs and symptoms of trauma in adolescence.

According to Kline and Levine, teens tend to do everything in their power to avoid the triggering feelings and thoughts that live with them from their traumatic event. This may make perfect sense for those reading this book as it may be hard to understand why they do some of the things they do. Compound their unhealthy behaviors like risky sexual activity, drugs, alcohol, and thrill-seeking with the sociopolitical development of their neighborhoods, and you have what we are seeing in Philadelphia, where the mayor is seen throwing up his hands and stating that he is so sick of having to deal with gun violence issues, that he will be glad to not be mayor anymore. The violence and chaos almost seem inevitable, and the amount of money the city has spent addressing it seems to not be working.

A way to alleviate the city would be to consider the interpersonal neuroscience of adolescence and understand how environments can determine which genes are expressed. When they created the "hood," they structurally designed it to allow easy access to unhealthy coping. However, we must not overlook the ways in which Black teens cope just because we may not agree. They flooded (filled) the hood with drugs, guns, and corner stores passed off as grocery stores which do not leave room for healthier alternatives. Yet, there are other ways to help your mental and physical wellness with managing anger.

In this chapter, we will introduce some positive ways to release anger through the benefits of a healthy diet, physical activity and movement, sleep, and positive relationships with a trusted adult. Kline and Levine created a Teen Trauma Symptom[34] Checklist on page 67:

34. Levine, P., & Kline, M. (2015). Trauma Through a Child's Eyes: Awakening the Ordinary Miracle of Healing. *Education Review, 0.* doi:http://dx.doi.org/10.14507/er.v0.844

- Abrupt changes in relationships, like sudden disinterest in favorite people
- Becoming detached and withdrawn
- Radical changes in grades, life attitudes, and/or appearance
- Sudden changes in behavior like life-threatening re-enactment or other acting-out
- Sudden changes in mood, especially anxiety, depression, and thoughts of suicide
- Dependency on alcohol and drugs
- Sudden disinterest in favorite hobbies or sports
- Irritability, anger, and the desire to take revenge
- Sexual promiscuity

Some, if not all, of the behaviors mentioned in their checklist could sum up the numerous headlines regarding violence in Philadelphia. For what it is worth, it highlights the importance of taking a deeper look at their behaviors because some could be linked to trauma and their difficulty in navigating it.

Here's the thing, no one is exempt from the unknowns and upsets of life. Black boys and men are forced to live under highly oppressive conditions without support. They abide by a social contract of toxic masculinity that not asking for help, or that receiving help, shows weakness.

Expressing emotion is a unit of measurement regarding masculinity, taking care of others before you take care of yourself, and so on, as the American dream. In my opinion, the socialization of masculinity and gender in America creates suicide because it ostracizes people into believing that the only way to make it through life is by yourself. Or as my best friend likes to call it, "The island of separation."

This island has become a place of vacation for Black boys and men. A place where they go when life is becoming heavy. What they do when reaching this island looks different per person. Also, every Black man's island may have different characteristics pertaining to the weather, environmental aspects, food, etc.

As a caring, you are probably wondering, how do I help them when they are on this island, or help them find their way back home? You must first practice and model what it looks like to navigate anger in a way that is safe for everybody and then provide him with the tools and resources to feel capable of managing his anger. Below are some ways to help:

Running: Initially, when you think of running, you probably think of exercise. Although exercise is essential, I am referring to something else. I am referencing the act of running, meaning what it represents. For example, running represents movement in a specific direction and a release from your body (i.e., sweat). When I run, I envision myself moving toward that person I see myself as and releasing the current things holding me back (i.e., anger). I use running to healthily remove the things stopping me from being my best self and kind to others. In other words, I run towards and through the anger, hurt, sadness, etc., instead of shying away.

Healthy Eating: If you don't remember anything else from this chapter, try to understand that everything is connected, meaning your brain, heart, gut, etc., are all connected and communicate with each other. There is a lot of research correlating mood and gut. Experts like Daniel Siegel believe that we have multiple brains, and the first is our gut. We have a neuro-network around our gut,[35] in which research suggests that there are 100 million nerve cells lining your gut. If you ever felt "butter-flies[36]" when you were nervous or went with a "gut feeling," then you know what I mean.

Ninety percent[37] of serotonin is in your gut. Serotonin is the hormone associated with feelings of happiness, focus, and calm. Psychotropics such as SSRIs, which stands for Selective Serotonin Reuptake Inhibitors, are used to help those diagnosed with depression, anxiety, and other mood-related disorders all seek to increase the level of serotonin within the brain (i.e., increase mood). Here's the connection- if ninety percent of serotonin is in your gut and SSRI medication was created to increase the amount of serotonin in the brain, the question then is where is the medication getting serotonin? The answer: the gut, which clearly explains the reasoning for common side effects of SSRIs being irritable bowel syndrome, nausea, and loss of appetite. The side effects of SSRI medication are indigestion, diarrhea, constipation, loss of appetite, weight loss, etc. I share this with the hopes that it makes you reconsider or carefully consider other ways to help your moody teen. Something as simple as a diet change may positively affect their mood.

Sleep: Most of all, make sure your teen gets enough sleep. Sleep deprivation can increase stress, mood swings, and irritability and cause weight, memory, concentration, and decision-making problems. Do not let your teen convince you that they function perfectly fine from a few hours of sleep, as most teens will

35. https://www.science.org/content/article/your-gut-directly-connected-your-brain-newly-discovered-neuron-circuit
36. https://www.hopkinsmedicine.org/health/wellness-and-prevention/the-brain-gut-connection
37. https://www.health.harvard.edu/blog/gut-feelings-how-food-affects-your-mood-2018120715548

debate. That is simply not healthy and not true. All teens should get between 8-10 hours of sleep. To achieve this, remove electronics or have them turn them off a couple hours before bedtime. Have them implement some of the meditation practices or affirmations found at the end of this book.

Key Takeaways:

- The adolescent period is a chaotic and confusing time before the trauma

- Teens will do everything in their power to avoid re-experiencing emotions, feelings, and thoughts like thrill-seeking behaviors

- Things like exercise, sleep, and healthy eating can play a huge role in assisting them to cope with life stressors

- Their environment plays a huge role in their exhibiting behavior

- City-wide supports need to understand the neuroscience of the adolescent brain and body to address issues like violence

- Implementing healthier ways for them to release their emotions, feelings, and thoughts instead of running away from them has the potential to help them grow into healthy coping adults

9

Connect • Compassion • Co-conspirator

The 3Cs

As a parent, teacher, educator, etc., your number one priority is the child. Yet, throughout our respective supportive roles, we often focus less on this vital factor and more on data, statistics, numbers, etc. As a therapeutic educator, I have learned that we have it backward. We were instructed or socialized to believe that good grades stem from good teaching or that a child can follow directions because they had a good leader.

Throughout my work, I have managed to relieve Black boys' and men's symptoms just after the first session or the first time meeting them. This had nothing to do with how good of a therapist or coach I am and everything to do with my ability to build a relationship. The relationship is where healing happens, meaning I was able to get them to move in a health-promoting direction, not because I am a firm believer in holistic modalities and against medications, but because I understand the importance of relationships.

No matter how good of a parent, teacher, educator, etc., you may be, if you cannot build a foundational relationship with Black male teens, then you will never have success. It is critical to understand that whether you are trying to teach a new concept, get them to learn a new sport, or manage their emotions, it all depends on the relationships. None of this can be understood outside the context of the relationship. So, it is not that the teacher did a poor job at teaching because the students failed. The teacher did a poor job of building a relationship with their students and pointed to a reason why the students failed.

Let's look at Bob, a brand-new Latin teacher at an all-boys school that is predominantly Black. Bob did not take any training regarding how to teach Latin, nor was it his passionate dream to become a Latin teacher. Given this information, we expect Bob to be a horrible Latin teacher. However, he became one of the student's favorite teachers. Why is this? He focused more on building relationships in ways the students preferred, like unique handshakes and greetings, allowing the students to decide what they wanted to learn regarding the subject matter, including their culture into the lesson plans, etc. Bob goes above and beyond to create and maintain a healthy, loving-kind relationship with his students.

Sounds simple right? The key is consistency. Black male teens receive consistent messaging that they are not worth it or no one cares, so to combat this constant negative messaging, one must put in double the work. Think of the guys who hug your neighborhood corners. One might call them drug dealers, thugs, etc., which is beside the point. They are effective because they faithfully chill on the same corner every day. This communicates that no matter the weather, circumstance, etc., they will always be there for you. If you ask me, they have the best business strategy regarding customer service.

The idea of healthy, safe, loving relationships is becoming more evident in its importance. If not, take a few of the cases from Dr. Bruce Perry's *The Boy Who Was Raised As A Dog*, where he was called to help children who suffered from a lack of healthy relationships. One of the children in the book, Leon, had been convicted of a capital offense and faced the death penalty. Leon's story is fascinating and highlights the impact of parental/caregiver neglect. Leon was considered a psychopath and did not express remorse for his behavior. The chapter is titled "The Coldest Heart," which implies the type of person Leon presented as.

Dr. Perry discovered that his lack of love during his developmental years resulted in his inability to feel or understand love. The story of Leon ends with him being executed. Leon was left alone for hours as a child, internalizing that no one would soothe his tears or meet his needs. Leon's case may sound extreme, but the importance of relationships should be taken very seriously. As Diane Wagenhals once said, "Change takes place in the context of relationships over time."

Okay, Kenn, we get it. It's all about relationships, but how do we build this type of foundation if we have never had it ourselves or seen it before? I am glad you asked! One aspect of Bourne Anew LLC is training organizations on how to do this exact thing. The way I train leaders is grounded in a framework that I call the 3Cs: Connect, Compassion, and Co-conspirator. This framework is one I have tested repeatedly, and it works. It is anti-racist, culturally congruent, anti-oppressive, and heart and experience centered. No matter the race, gender, sexual orientation, socioeconomic status, or any other difference, effectively implementing the 3Cs will take your relationship-building skills with Black male teens to the next level.

Before I explain the 3Cs, I must review a trauma framework called the 3Rs. The 3Rs are: Regulate, Relate, and Reason. These are steps that trauma-informed care practitioners use when working with individuals impacted by trauma—the 3Rs work parallel with the brain, meaning bottom up. The brain is developed bottom up, starting with the brainstem and advancing to the cortex region; recall the information discussed in Chapter Five. The brainstem is responsible for autonomic functions like heart rate, breathing, etc. This area of the brain is essential regarding relationships because when people are overwhelmed, they tend to work their way down to lower brain regions.

If we want to **connect** with people during a triggering experience, we must understand where they are to help. There is a saying in social work that says, "Meet people where they are," and understanding how people respond to being overwhelmed can help you meet them where they are. Specifically, Black male teens tend to react from their lowest brain region (i.e., brainstem) when they are overwhelmed with anger.

To be clear, when I mention the idea of one working their way down to lower brain regions, I am talking about a process that strictly happens on the inside and is natural. Imagine the brain as four Lego blocks, as discussed in chapter five. The first block, being the base, is the brainstem, followed by the midbrain, limbic, and cortex. As one becomes overwhelmed, imagine the Lego blocks disconnecting from the top until reaching the base. Some call it "flipping your lid."

Once your Black male teen experiences an overwhelming experience, a trauma-informed care practitioner should focus on the first R: regulate. Regulating speaks to this first Lego block of the brain and is essential in helping one return to a calm state. It is equally important that I mention that returning to a state of calm is natural and can only be done by the person. We can only help or hurt this process.

Assisting a person to regulate looks like mirroring calm-deep breaths, getting a drink of water, going for a walk, etc. These activities help regulate the fight, flight, or freeze responses that live within our lower brain regions. Other examples would be humming, doodling, and calming music. The trick is to communicate safety at this stage. Some things to NOT do andsay are: "Calm down!" Ask, "What's wrong with you?" Respond by yelling, reacting with violence, or calling the police. None of those things communicate safety, calm, or control to Black male teenagers, and if we are speaking scientifically, none of it express- es calm to anyone who is triggered. Remember, once a person is overwhelmed, they are most likely responding from a lower brain region which requires specific activities/words that com- municate to that region.

The 3Cs parallel the 3Rs and must be done in order as each C speaks to a particular brain region.

Connect:

The first is connect. Connecting is synonymous with Regulating, as it speaks to lower brain regions. The difference lies within the actions that come with connecting versus regulating. When your Black male teen is overwhelmed and angry, the first step is to *connect*. For clarification, anger is different from rage. Rage is a buildup of ignored anger and can seem quite explosive. Anger is a human emotion that comes and goes. Connecting mainly focuses on identifying with the subjective experience.

A subjective experience refers to the emotional and cogni- tive impact of a human experience as opposed to an objective experience which is the actual events of the experience. While something objective is tangible and can be experienced by oth- ers, subjective experiences are produced by the individual mind. At the same time, quite real to the person experiencing a sub- jective experience, and often profound others cannot objectively or empirically measure it. For instance, we all have a subjective experience whenever we are experiencing pain. Although we as an individual can identify and feel the specific components of the pain, no one else can fully measure or feel our own subjective experience of pain. So, the goal is to connect and identify with whatever Black male teens are expressing that they are feeling in a nonjudgmental manner. Non-judgmental includes facial expressions and remarks that say, "What do you mean," "It doesn't hurt that bad," "I feel your pain," or anything that dismisses how they feel. Connect with what they are feeling and not with what you understand regarding that feeling.

The focus is on them.

Clear your mind of anything else. If you can effectively complete this, you will be able to talk a person off a ledge. So, how does connecting look and sound? In achieving the first c, one must only work with whatever is. So, if they say they feel hurt, then that's what you identify with. This can be understood more clearly through the following example: Have you ever asked someone how they are, and they replied with "good." Typically, the conversation ends here as you respond with "that's good" or "good to hear." But if you are seeking to identify with their subjective experience, this same interaction would look and sound more like:

"Hey, how are you?"

"I'm doing good; how about you?"

"I really care about your well-being, so when you say you are doing good, I am not sure what that means because good is not a feeling. Help me understand what good means for you?"

Here the difference lies in the reality that the first example clearly does not show interest or care in wanting to know how the person was feeling and the second example seeks to understand fully. This is important because Black male teens will test you with this "I'm good" saying to see if you care. Once you respond with "That's good," you lose them, and they quickly determine that you were being polite and only spoke to them because you felt like that was the right thing to do.

In working with someone who is demonstrating that they are overwhelmed and having completed the first phase, a trauma-informed care practitioner would then move to the next R, which relates. Relating looks like a safe, trustworthy adult to help re-establish safety. This adult may say things like, "I see you are upset," or "I am here when you're ready to talk."

The problem with this phase is that it is moving too quickly. In only completing phase one and now reaching the second or third Lego block (i.e., limbic system and midbrain), these brain regions are not responsible for coherent thought, logic, or even language. So, telling a person who is overwhelmed, "I am here when you are ready to talk," does nothing for the individual because they do not feel they will ever be ready to talk.

Also, these second and third Lego blocks or brain regions cannot think/perform beyond seconds and minutes. A person functioning from their midbrain and limbic area can think only seconds, minutes, and sometimes an hour ahead. Things seem urgent and need to be addressed right now. These second and third Lego blocks focus more on emotions and memory. So, as an adult, you need to communicate how they are feeling. This is where the second C comes in.

Compassion:

The Latin root for the word compassion is *pati*, which means *to suffer*. The prefix com means *with*. So, in having **compassion** for Black male teens, we must suffer with them. How I use the term compassion is different from empathy or altruism. The second C within the 3Cs requires investment and collective action.

Compassion rests in the idea that I am invested in your well-being, and we can do something about it together. This is not feeling sorry for someone or simply wanting to help because you feel like you can alleviate what they are going through and, in turn, stroke your ego that says you're a good person.

One way to show compassion in this manner is through love. Through love, we regulate each other's brain chemistry, sense of well-being, and immunological functioning. And when love is thwarted through things like abuse and neglect, our mental health is compromised. This is aligned with social work's core values of dignity and worth of a person, and by knowing that just by loving them, you are making a difference towards their mental health.

Another thing about compassion and why we need to suffer with someone is that we tend not to care until it hits home. But if we truly understand our relationship to one another and the planet, then you would be able to see the connection of how we are all in this together. Be careful with this, as there is a fine line between being overwhelmed and feeling someone else's pain. This must be done through open awareness. Open awareness refers to being receptive to objects within awareness without getting attached to or lost in them.

So how does *compassion* look or sound? In trying to feel the suffering of another or suffer with another, I urge extreme caution and to seek professional help as this can be triggering and unsafe for you to do on your own. One way I do this for my clients is through body scans. Body scans are a somatic therapeutic tool to help one become more in tune with what they are feeling and where they are feeling it. This can be accomplished by paying attention to yourself on a deeper level that allows you to pinpoint exactly where your feelings or trauma resides in your body. I complete body scans as a meditation-type practice where I have them close their eyes, sit upright, their feet planted on the ground, and their bodies open (no crossed arms or legs). I then start from their toes and slowly work our way up to the tops of our heads. This exercise does two things: 1) shows them that they can control their attention and where it goes, and 2) notice bodily sensations with loving-kindness.

Co-conspirator

The third c is **Co-conspirator** which parallels the third r, which is reason. Reason is parallel with the top lego block or the cortex brain region. Here we have logic, reasoning, coherent thoughts, etc. So, a trauma-informed care professional should allow for reflection for the purposes of learning how to do better next time. Some language or questions that may be said or asked are "What triggered you," "How can you approach this trigger in the future so that you feel safe" and "How can others approach this trigger in the future to help you feel safe?"

In line with this thinking, the third c, which is a co-conspirator, goes a step beyond reflection. In my framework, a co-conspirator reflects on the trigger but then seeks to restore well-being and power by realizing that one's symptoms are always rooted in a system. Whatever it was that overwhelmed him can also be connected to a larger system that seeks to destroy him mentally. Black male teens are at war with themselves and the rest of society as they are trying to figure it all out. Allowing him to address his triggers and take action in making lasting changes for himself and his community can genuinely empower an individual.

This could look like having them participate in anti-gun projects, protests, civil action, etc., after you notice that they have had a hard time dealing with their friend's death. See, this step goes beyond only acknowledging that they are having a hard time. It helps them name their feelings, reflect, identify their triggers, identify the systems at play, and restore their well-being and power by motivating them to participate in key events that can make a difference for them and those they love. Also, this step requires that you (the adult) be an active member in this process, so much so that a person on the outside should not be able to tell who is more passionate. As Black folks say, "You gotta put some skin in the game!"

As an adult, you must show that you are in this just as much as they are, and one way to do that is by answering the question, what are you willing to lose for lasting systemic change? At this point, you have enough information to guide a Black male teen to a place where they can find meaning in moving toward healing. Essentially, they are the coach, and you're the assistant coach. The team needs both of y'all.

The questions you're asking should be directly related to an action plan for both of all of you. This is your foundation for dismantling, combating, and creating lasting change!

Key Takeaways:

- Identify with their subjective experience: recognize and acknowledge whatever they say they feel.

- Learn how to suffer with an individual versus feeling sorry for them.

- Be about that action. Don't just say, "I am here when you need me," but instead, be invested just as much as them.

- Healthy, safe, and loving relationships can and will make a difference.

- Relationships are where healing happens.

Conclusion

I n summation, understanding anger as an emotion and treating it as such can be beneficial, keeping in mind that our emotions are here to guide us. No one is right or wrong in expressing emotion. They are simply human. The difference lies in how one expresses such emotions and how one navigates an emotion. Anger - the word emotion is derived from the Latin word *emovere*. *Emovere* means to move or move out. Essentially emotion is the process that evokes motion. In defining *anger*, we suggest symptoms or descriptions rooted in some form of motion or drive to do something. Anger is often the emotion Black teens are taught to express.

Exploring the underlying causes of anger can help Black teens identify their needs. Anger in America has been used as a systemic tool to label our Black teens, further causing more harm and justification for violence against them. Emotions and feelings are what make us human and should not be punished. A huge part of helping your teen is also helping yourself. Understanding the root causes of your emotions and practicing how to communicate them effectively will directly affect your teen's ability to do the same. An adult's capacity to restore equilibrium quickly and naturally to our nervous systems and build our capacity for a resilient nervous system is critical, so we can bend without breaking. To support and serve your teen experiencing anger, you must learn to attune to your own sensations, rhythms, and emotions.

In discussing one's emotions, the words right or wrong should not be mentioned because there is no right or wrong way to feel. Think of emotions as a car: When such emotion comes up, it should be seen as a signal to pull over and check underneath the hood. Keeping in mind that teenagers' brains are going through profound changes, making them susceptible to mental health challenges, punishing them for emotion will further harm their development. Their emotions should be explored and used to bring about change. Instead, they are learning to suppress their emotions due to society's negative outlook on Black boys.

As we say in social work, "the personal is political," which means one's personal life is influenced and sometimes determined by their environment, laws, politics, and unspoken social contracts. Subscribing to manhood or ideals of what being a man consist, needs to be aligned with who they feel they are and not what society implies. Our heteronormative patriarchal society believes white men to be the standard. This is problematic for Black male teens because what we are essentially communicating is that, they will never be a man or seen as one because our current definition of being a man is rooted in racism. Subscribing to this definition causes more stress because we, as Black men, will never be afforded access to systems of privilege as our counterparts. If you do not remember anything from this book but one thing, please remember that healthy, safe, loving relationships can help Black male teens express and communicate their emotions and restore their well-being.

Appendix: A Chapter To Go Over With Your Parents and Educators To Help Them Best Support You

The purpose of this chapter is to empower teens to have conversations with the adults in their lives about their anger and how they need support.

This is not solely your fault; you are doing the best you can with your knowledge, know-how, and tools. How you were raised by your parents, who their elders raised, potentially has been perpetuating unhealthy developmental behaviors for a very long time. As once a school social worker at a Black all-boys school in West Philadelphia, street leader director in Camden, New Jersey, and a community intervention specialist with Drexel University, I must admit that our parents, educators, and members alike are too a part of the problem. They are not the only issue but play a significant role in the behaviors you see today.

As a Black male teen, this may be hard to comprehend but trust that they are doing the best they can with the coping skills that they have. Below you will find some helpful language, tools, and resources that you can use to help get the support you need. Do not forget that the other tools mentioned in this book should also be used.

Tools To Use With Your Caregiver

"Hi, I'm looking for someone my son can talk to. He attends [a] university, and although I haven't been the best mom and my husband has not been the best dad, he's a good young adult, and I want to make sure he becomes a better man, not a bitter man."

Remember, children are not our property, but our responsibility in ensuring their healthy development. I understand that our laws may communicate and perpetuate this idea. However, responsibility is not the same as ownership. You are responsible for watering and caring for the seed (Black male teen) you were given. We cannot determine the type of flower that will grow. As a caregiver, teacher, etc., here are some DON'TS when helping a Black male teenager:

Escalating The Situation

- Remember, it is not about you or what you perceive but about them and how they feel. Simply staying with this reality can help you not take it personally when their behaviors may feel like disrespect.

Threatening Consequences

- Do not use punishment as your first, second, or third option when providing discipline. Lead with love. Unknowingly, you could be punishing him for having gone through a traumatic experience or expressing emotion.

Physically Intervening

- Never result in using physical contact when intervening. The first step in intervening should be to communicate to his body and mind that he is safe, and if you use physical contact, it will communicate the exact opposite and exacerbate his symptoms.

Getting the Last Word

- As much as he feels like he knows everything and always has to say something in response to what you said, know that this is a part of finding his voice. It is not to "get smart" or "talk back." It is simply them trying to find their voice and learn how to communicate. If you shut this down, then later in life, it may show up as low self-esteem or poor communication within their relationships.

Not Sticking to the Facts

- Perception is everything. This is not a battle of how you see it versus how they see it. Make sure your understanding is in alignment with their reality. If your understanding is not aligned with their reality, then you must make sure you stick to the facts which are their reality.

Tips and strategies for caregivers

- *Be a role model for your teen. Help decode anger*
  - o Our brains have mirror neurons, and mirroring what you want your Black male teen to do is a way to help them figure out their anger.

- *Give your teen time and space to calm down*
  - o The actual space in which the altercation has taken place is now a place that does not communicate safety to them and will continue to trigger them, so allowing them to leave that space and go somewhere else (i.e., another room, outside for a walk, etc.) can help communicate to their body that they are safe.

- *Avoid power struggles*
  - o We are all humans that need love, compassion, care, and kindness. When dealing with Black male teens' emotions, it matters not your authority or role but how much you can let go of that authority and power and communicate love.

- *Encourage your teen to communicate their emotions*
  - o Always validate and never question. Asking a Black male teen, "Why do you feel that way," can be received as judgment. Just listen and validate. No matter your views on the situation. Feelings and emotions are not meant to be judged nor need to exist within categories of right or wrong.

- *Set up rules and consequences in advance*
  - o Boundaries are meant to keep everyone safe. Contrary to popular belief, they are not meant to offend. Establishing clear boundaries and allowing room for those boundaries to be flexible over time is key

- *Reach out*
  - o Do not overlook your teens' emotions. Offer a compassionate ear or concerned heart and see what has been happening to them. Refer to the Compassion section in Chapter Nine.

- *Validate and show respect*
  - o Let go of the idea "one has to give respect in order to receive." Respect is a human right, not a privilege.

- *Check-in with yourself*
  - o This stuff is hard work. You can only give what you are filled with. Fill yourself with the same love and kindness that you are showing your Black male teen.

Things to Share with your Educators

Schools should foster community and healthy relationships.

The curriculum should help students work together versus compete. Policies involving school discipline, authorities, staff, etc., should require implicit bias training and workshops led by Black men passionate about that work. If you are an educator and do not know where to find this resource, I can help you. I provide some of these resources but also know other Black men who are excellent at what they do.

Whether you realize it or not, everyone has bias, and it must be addressed, especially when working with Black male teens. "Black male students are less likely to feel motivated to invest in school when they don't feel as if the teachers care about them... even studies done on Black males in suburban areas concluded the same findings.[38] It is more about the relationship and what Black male teens can feel or sense from the relationship than it is about education. If they feel that you truly care, then teaching will come easy.

This last section is strictly for the Black male teen in your life. I created an affirmation guide to help them as they grow on their journey.

---

38. Lynn, et al., (2010). Examining Teachers' Beliefs about African American Male Students in a Low-Performing High School in an African American School District. Teachers College Record, v112 n1 p289-330

A Beginner's Guide To Affirmations for Black Males

This section was added in response to many clients needing to learn or never hearing about the power of affirmations. The purpose of this section is to provide the reader with a starting point and a how-to road map regarding affirmations. The following strategies were created with my Black male clients in mind. The categories of affirmations are organized as the most common issues my clients struggled with. In addition, the categories come from frequent inquiries when requesting help.

I analyzed over 100 inquiries regarding my services and found the themes within them. However, I did not just want to create a resource with a list of affirmations—it needed to be thorough and backed by research. All ideas discussed throughout this guide are supported by research and lived experiences. I hope this guide leads Black men and the global majority on their healing journeys.

> *A Letter From My True Self,*
>
> *Do you remember always being asked, "Why are you so mad," in joking tones? You hid me behind laughter and anger. I tried being there for you the best I could, but you became numb to me over time. I tried to come out in tears or through hugs, but you didn't let me. You told me I was fat and ugly, that no girl I would ever want would like me and that they would only like me because*

I am funny. You covered me in oversized clothes but continued to feed me fat-inducing foods. You blasted my ears with music filled with hate, killing, and selfless acts. You stopped talking to me when you stopped going to church. You were very hurtful to those around you because you were never taught or shown an example of love that made sense. You were never given the words to express love or even say the words "I love you." You were taught lies, manipulation, and negative self-talk. You were shown how to run away when things got tough. **You were told never to let anyone disrespect you; if they do, you must inflict physical harm. Hurt people hurt people disguised as culture.** *But I was always there. Like when I stood up for the kid around the corner because he was getting bullied for his size. We almost fought that whole block that day. What about when you checked the guy who was disrespecting the bike store employee by calling her out of her name? We managed to calm him down, resulting in no cops being called and no one getting hurt. That random act of kindness when you made that guy feel seen who later shared that he had just got out of prison, and you were the first person to acknowledge him. Being thanked by the guy who was diagnosed with schizophrenia for letting him speak and be listened to. You got the guy's dietary needs adhered to in the correctional facility, made friends with those the system labels "less fortunate" to the point where they were giving you items of their bodies (sunglasses) as a thank you, held mom when she was crying, always interjected when they were fighting, and so many other moments. How come I couldn't develop and grow?*

I added this piece of vulnerability as I felt that so many of us are hiding our true selves. This happens to survive our violently structured environments that do not support the loving-kind people we indeed are. I leave this piece of me with you to show that I am no different or better, and I hope this will help create some trust as you move throughout this guide. I hope this will free your true self from that dark place it's been hiding.

As one of the few cisgender heterosexual Black male therapeutic educators in Philadelphia, Pennsylvania, who works with adults and teens, I have a passion and heart to connect with those who want better for themselves but have been systemically mind-f*cked to think otherwise. I was born in Philadelphia and raised in Southwest Philadelphia.

I learned early on about the structurally designed mishaps that built my community to further a white supremacist agenda. In other words, the hood was designed for capitalist reasons and not because of culture. I did what I had to for survival, but I always knew that there was more to life than what my environment presented. There were no positive role models, roadmaps, or guidance on how to create the life you want. This book serves as all the above for those with odds stacked against them but won't quit.

After attaining my master's degree in social work, I worked several jobs in which I served the global majority. I began to see trends within the inquiries for therapy. Whether I received an email, phone call, word of mouth, etc., folks (typically Black women- mom, grandmom, sister, partner, or loved one) were all inquiring about similar services.

Being a Black male in America takes a heavy toll on your being. It means to be attacked mentally, physically, spiritually, and humanly. Who do we turn to when we just want to sort through it all? Is there anyone who truly cares that will understand what we go through? Every inquiry asked for help with the following areas:

- Anger
- Grief
- Loss
- Depression
- Anxiety
- Relationships
- Trauma
- Substance use
- Thinks no one will understand
- Wanting a better life

When asked, "have you ever heard of affirmations" or "speaking kindly to yourself," the answer was often *no.* This guide was designed to help remind you of all that you know you are. It was designed to shine a light on that dark part within your soul where your true self hides. The only requirement is that you open this book as much as you do your phone and believe in the power of words.

To give you some context regarding the power of words, we will consider some thought-provoking questions that will make you rethink words and the power they hold:

When you say hurtful things to others, where do you think the words go?

When someone says something hurtful to you, where do the words live?

How do you listen to others? Do you find that you listen to certain individuals differently than others?

What does "in one ear and out the other" mean? And once it goes through your ears, where does it pass through? Your brain?

The goal is to simply urge you to consider that the words we speak out of our mouths hold a deeper meaning. Keep this idea in your mind as you read this book. Your life can significantly be happier and healthier with daily practice in stopping your overwhelming negative thoughts and replacing them with affirmations.

Words and thoughts have a vibrational frequency that likes to attract likeness. Speak kindly to yourself and attract kindness. Speak love to yourself and attract love. Speak and think loving-kindness and enjoy the peace that will come with it.

Brain Basics

This section gives you a basic understanding of what may be happening internally, so that you can feel more equipped to change what's happening externally. In other words, as the great Maya Angelou once said, "When you know better, you do better."

I hypothesize that the idea of low self-esteem lives within the limbic area of our brains. The limbic area is responsible for how we experience and express emotions and motivation and determines whether things are good or bad. Low self-esteem usually presents as an emotion that grows from our perception of something being bad or not good enough, resulting in low motivation. It is essential to add that within the limbic area exist the amygdala and hippocampus.

To keep it brief, the amygdala acts as a router, constantly scanning the world and determining where that information goes (i.e., to other parts of the brain). It can hijack the part of your brain responsible for making logical decisions if there is enough emotional charge created by incoming data. In this case, the person will react out of pure emotion or survival. The hippocampus stores images and facts so that if something familiar happens, it triggers the memories it has stored. Both the amygdala and hippocampus communicate with each other to determine how the brain should respond in any given situation.

For example, let's say you were cheated on in a past relationship. Your amygdala received this emotionally charged (as behaviors, words, smells, etc.) event, while your hippocampus stored images and facts from this event. You begin to internalize this citation and replay it over and over in your head, to the point where you somehow find a way to blame yourself as the cause of your ex's actions. Feelings of embarrassment, hurt, shame, guilt, etc. takeover, and now your body has developed a reaction to relationships. It is important to note that everything I just described happens at a speed that you do not realize it's happening. Remember that the amygdala is where fear, learned from past experiences, is permanently stored. Fast forward to your current relationship, where similar words and behaviors begin to show, triggering your amygdala and hippocampus to perceive this current situation as the last painful relationship, automatically triggering feelings of embarrassment, hurt, shame, guilt, etc. Now, you're emotionally reactive to your partner because you perceive that things are going downhill.

Meanwhile, a simple conversation could have taken place to fact-check your perceptions. You did not have a conversation with your partner because whenever you first experienced that situation, your brain and body embedded a response. Whatever that response was is how you show up in every similar situation unless you actively work at rewiring this embedded response.

Safety Plan

When you're a caregiver, you need to realize that you've got to take care of yourself because not only are you going to have to rise to the occasion and help someone else, but you must model for the next generation. -Naomi Jedd

As a therapeutic educator, one of my jobs is to ensure your safety when possible. Knowing that this information can trigger unwanted feelings and behaviors, we must take the time to create a safety plan before moving forward in this book. Lakeside Global Institute defines a safety plan as *a predetermined list of ways a person can mentally or physically ensure they remain safe, especially if a topic, activity, or environment is perceived as potentially dangerous or threatening"* (Enhancing Trauma Awareness, pg. 8).

There are two types of safety plans: 1) internal and 2) external. An internal safety plan highlights things a person can do to stay calm mentally. An external safety plan focuses on taking necessary physical action to create safety. Please create both or have a little bit of both within your safety plan. To help you get started, please refer to Figures 1 and 1A below.

Figure 1. Self-Care Plan Example: Internal

☐ Name one thing I can see. ☐ Name one thing I can smell. ☐ Name one thing I can touch. ☐ Name one thing I can taste.	☐ I am safe. ☐ I am loved. ☐ I have the power to care for myself. ☐ I am not in danger.
☐ Intentionally feel my drawers touch my skin. ☐ Breathe. Slowly. Deeply. ☐ Remind yourself of the date and time.	☐ What am I feeling? ☐ Where am I feeling it? ☐ How can I regain a sense of calm?

Figure 1A Self-Care Plan Example: External

☐ Note where exits are. ☐ Sit near the door. ☐ Notice who is in the room. ☐ Tell someone you trust when you start to feel unsafe.	☐ Sit near someone you feel safe being close to. ☐ Go to the bathroom. ☐ Sit in a spot where you feel safest. ☐ Decide a safe place to go.
☐ Doodle ☐ Quietly humming ☐ Tapping ☐ Think about what you will eat as your next meal	☐ Drink water. ☐ Exit the room. ☐ Refuse to speak. ☐ Close your eyes for a few seconds.

Your safety is a priority. Take an index card and create a safety plan using figures 1 and 1A. Do this before moving forward in this book. This will better prepare you for unwarranted emotions, feelings, and thoughts. I suggest using this index card as a bookmark so that you have it readily available in case you need it.

This affirmation guide has nine sections: 1) *Inner Child* 2) *Past Mistakes* 3) *Trauma* 4) *Better Quality of Life* 5) *Anger* 6) *Depression* 7) *Anxiety* 8) *Grief* 9) *Relationships*

1. *Inner Child:* seeks to speak to your inner child in hopes of soothing the hurt that was done.

2. *Past Mistakes:* Letting go of regret and not allowing your past to stop you from doing your best.

3. *Trauma:* Soothing your survival brain.

4. *Better Quality of Life:* Attaining inner peace

5. *Anger:* How to manage it.

6. *Depression:* Deep sadness that affects day-to-day life

7. *Anxiety:* Overwhelming emotions

8. *Grief:* Loss of loved ones and old lifestyle

9. *Relationships:* With self and others (romantically and non-romantically)

These nine sections serve as the umbrellas that blocked the sunshine within my adult clients. These are the top reasons in which Black boys/men inquire about services at Bourne Anew LLC. For the purposes of this book, I only highlight the anger section. This complete guide can be found at www.bourneanew. com or email me at bourneanewllc@bourneanew.com and state that you have read this book and are looking for the complete affirmation guide.

Anger

How to manage

- I will no longer be controlled by anger.
- I understand that anger is just an emotion.
- I am learning to listen and feel my emotions instead of numbing them.
- I now realize that being angry is a reminder that I am human.
- I am allowed to be angry.
- I refuse to let anger take control of my life.
- I decide how I will react or respond to a situation and not my anger.
- I recognize what triggers my anger and will use my safety plan to create peace for myself.

- I am capable of de-escalating any situation with compassion, understanding, and patience.
- I am becoming a better version of myself and will treat others with kindness.
- I remain present within triggering situations.
- I define who I am.
- I am peace.
- I am love.
- I will react from a space of love and kindness.
- I embrace the discomfort and tension to learn more about myself.
- I can remain calm.
- I refuse to let anger steal my inner peace.
- I am freeing up space within my heart to receive more joy and happiness.
- I have all the tools to change my life.
- I am committed to my inner peace.
- I welcome people and experiences that bring me joy.
- I can feel my anger and keep control.
- I can express and communicate my anger in a safe, respectful way.
- I release all this built-up anger.

Action Plan:

Emovere:

Here are some practical ways to implement affirmations. The key to affirmations and speaking kindly to yourself is the action you take following the affirmation. This is important because when it comes to emotions, another important detail to understand is the word emotion is derived from the Latin word *emovere.* Trust me on this– I took honors Latin all four years of high school. *Emovere* means to move or move out. Essentially emotion is the process that evokes motion. These emotional sparks of movement can be interpreted as passion if we see them that way. So, what motion will you be taking after reading these affirmations? What are you moving out?

How to use these affirmations to take action:

> *"I have the power to control my response to the emotions I feel."*

Actionable Plan:

Here are two actionable options you can create a habit with:

1. Complete a light two-minute meditation in the morning and before bed.
2. Sit still and do nothing for one- minute

Here is an example of a light two-minute meditation from start to finish:

Tools Needed: Music, room, and yourself

- Phone, computer, TV, etc. (any device that can access the internet or music streaming service)

- 7.83hz Schumann resonance playing in the background at a comfortable volume that blocks out the noise around you (search: 7.83hz Schuman resonance). Pick a video or song that sounds pleasing to you.

- Find a room/place/space that reminds you of peace, communicates safety to your body, and provides privacy for the time being with no interruptions (yes, this can be the bathroom), preferably somewhere in nature

- Close your eyes

- As you are sitting in silence, focus on your breath.

  o Take deep breaths (in through your nose 4s, hold your breath 4s, and exhale out of your mouth for 6s.

  o Repeat this type of breathing until your shoulders fall, your tongue rest behind the bottom teeth row, and you fully melt into the surface supporting you.

Your goal will determine the meditation and what you will say, but for the purposes of this book, we will provide you with a script

- Pick an affirmation and repeat it to yourself. Out loud or in your mind
- Example: Anxiety Affirmation number 8 says *I will be okay*.
- Repeat this affirmation over and over to yourself and allow the emotions to rise and fall.

*Important note: Have your safety plan nearby, as doing these types of meditations can be emotionally heavy.

Pro tip:

Try this quick and easy meditation called "Thank you."
Follow all the steps above and replace doing nothing with this bodily gesture:

- Right hand on the left shoulder and left hand on the right shoulder or upper arm (your arms should make an X - cross arms)
- Like you're hugging yourself
- And listen to an uplifting song: try this: Beautiful chorus group - inner peace (YouTube)

Here is an example of what your morning could look like:

- DO NOT grab your phone. Instead, grab your bible or journal and write out your thoughts that have been keeping you up at night. Also, write down your dreams and visions
- Make sure to include some affirmations from above in your journal or prayer.
- Complete some stretches. The goal is to do them slowly while breathing slowly.
- Wash your face. Breathe slowly as you wash your face. Slow down. There is no rush.
- Set your intentions for the day.
- Expect the unexpected and be kind to yourself as you navigate the day.

Affirmations can be a helpful tool in rewiring all the negative thinking we have of ourselves. It is not about saying random things that sound good but understanding the power that lies within you to change your life– recognizing the healing properties within our words and acting toward the life we want. We all long for happiness but seldom do we recognize the contrast that it is the sadness that makes happiness.

All of what you've been through has prepared you to continue your journey if you allow it– remembering that it is all connected and everything on earth was put here for your benefit. I wish you nothing but wellness and moments filled with happiness as you recognize the light within you.

Bibliography

Ackerman S. Discovering the Brain. Washington (DC): National Academies Press (US); 1992. 6, The Development and Shaping of the Brain. Available from: https://www.ncbi.nlm.nih.gov/books/NBK234146/

Barlow, D. H. (2004). Anxiety and its disorders: The nature and treatment of anxiety and panic. Guilford press.

Cozolino, Louis J., author. The Neuroscience of Human Relationships: Attachment and the Developing Social Brain. New York: W.W. Norton & Company, 2014.

Elgin, H.S. (1995). You Can't Say That To Me. (1st Edition).

Kalyani BG, Venkatasubramanian G, Arasappa R, Rao NP, Kalmady SV, Behere RV, Rao H, Vasudev MK, Gangadhar BN. Neurohemodynamic correlates of 'OM' chanting: A pilot functional magnetic resonance imaging study. Int J Yoga. 2011 Jan;4(1):3-6. doi: 10.4103/0973-6131.78171. PMID: 21654968; PMCID: PMC3099099.

Lakeside Global Institute, Deepening Trauma Awareness, (2006).

Lakeside Global Institute, Enhancing Trauma Awareness, (2006).

Levine P. A. & Kline M. (2019). Trauma through a child's eyes: awakening the ordinary miracle of healing. North Atlantic Books.

Lynn, et al., (2010). Examining Teachers' Beliefs about African American Male Students in a Low-Performing High School in an African American School District. Teachers College Record, v112 n1 p289-330

Menakem, R. (2017). *My grandmother's hands*. Central Recovery Press.

Mindsight Institute. (2019). Mindsightinstitute.com. https://www.mindsightinstitute.com/

Perry, B. D., & Szalavitz, M. (2007). *The boy who was raised as a dog*. Basic Books.

Poulin, J.-F., Caronia, G., Hofer, C., Cui, Q., Helm, B., Ramakrishnan, C., et al. (2018). Mapping projections of molecularly defined dopamine neuron subtypes using intersectional genetic approaches. Nat. Neurosci. 21, 1260–1271. doi: 10.1038/s41593-018-0203-4

Siegel, D. J. [Dr. Dan Siegel]. (2017 August 9). Dr. Dan Siegel's Hand Model of the Brain. [Video]. YouTube. https://www.youtube.com/watch?v=f-m2YcdMdFw

Wilson A. N. (2011). *Black-on-black violence: the psychodynamics of black self-annihilation in service of white domination* (2nd ed.). Afrikan World InfoSystems.

https://www.health.harvard.edu/blog/gut-feelings-how-food-affects-your-mood-2018120715548

https://www.hopkinsmedicine.org/health/wellness-and-prevention/the-brain-gut-connection

https://www.science.org/content/article/your-gut-directly-connected-your-brain-newly-discovered-neuron-circuit

https://www.slps.org/site/handlers/filedownload.ashx?moduleinstanceid=53801&dataid=47987&FileName=The%20Brain%20AA%202020%20Info%20Sheet.pdf